FRESH MANNA
JOURNEY TO A
NEW BEGINNING

FRESH MANNA
JOURNEY TO A NEW BEGINNING

SHAWANDA R. RANDOLPH

Fresh Manna: Journey To A New Beginning by
Shawanda R. Randolph

No part of this book may be reproduced in any written, electronic, recording, or photocopying without written permission of the publisher or author.

Scripture quotations marked NRSV are taken from the New Revised Standard Version of the Bible, copyright 1989, by the Division of Christian Education of the National Council of the Churches of Christ in the United States of America. Used by permission.

Scripture quotations marked MSG are taken from *The Message*. Copyright © 1993, 1994, 1995, 1996, 2000, 2001, 2002. Used by permission of NavPress Publishing Group.

Scripture quotations marked (NLT) are taken from the Holy Bible, New Living Translation, copyright © 1996, 2004, 2007, 2013, 2015 by Tyndale House Foundation. Used by permission of Tyndale House Publishers, Inc., Carol Stream, Illinois 60188. All rights reserved

Scripture quotations marked NIV are taken from THE HOLY BIBLE, NEW INTERNATIONAL VERSION®, NIV® Copyright © 1973, 1978, 1984, 2011 by Biblica, Inc.® Used by permission. All rights reserved worldwide.

Copyright © 2018 by Shawanda R. Randolph. All rights reserved.

Visit the author's Web site: Shawandarandolph.com

ISBN-13: 978-0-692-09754-0

For the lost,
    The sick,
        The hungry,
           The thirsty
                The uncovered
(naked)
                    The
unsheltered
    For you ARE God's chosen people

Table of Contents

PROLOGUE xi
MORE THAN JUST SOMEONE'S CHILD xiii
STAGE I: EVERYTHING YOU EVER NEED 1
   DAY ONE: TRUST GOD 3
   DAY TWO: TAKE A STAND 8
   DAY THREE: SHED and SURRENDER 11
   DAY FOUR: THE LIGHT WITHIN 13
   DAY FIVE: ANCHORS 15
STAGE II: WALK WITH ME 17
   DAY SIX: JUST A LITTLE FAITH 18
   DAY SEVEN: POSITIONING YOURSELF
   FOR BATTLE 21
   DAY EIGHT: CHAMPION 24
   DAY NINE: THE GATHERING 26
   DAY TEN: WHO HAS YOUR IDENTITY 30
STAGE III: DESTINY AWAITS 36
   DAY ELEVEN: SMALL BEGINNINGS 39
   DAY TWELVE: NEW VISION 42
   DAY THIRTEEN: BE YE DIFFERENT 47
   DAY FOURTEEN: WHAT IS YOUR SOURCE?
   50
   DAY FIFTEEN: DOUBLE LIFE 57
STAGE IV: ENJOY THE JOURNEY 64

- DAY SIXTEEN: NO UNDERDOGS HERE 66
- DAY SEVENTEEN: WHAT'S IT WORTH TO YOU? 70
- DAY EIGHTEEN: HE WILL WORK IT OUT .. 74
- DAY NINETEEN: THE GREATEST LOVE 78
- DAY TWENTY: PROMISES... PROMISES... PROMISES 84

STAGE V: COME...SEEK...FIND 88
- DAY TWENTY-ONE: WOLF OR SHEEP 90
- DAY TWENTY-TWO: COME OUT OF THE CLOSET 95
- DAY TWENTY-THREE: FOLLOWER OR DISCIPLE - WHICH ONE ARE YOU? 100
- DAY TWENTY-FOUR: WHAT DO YOU BELIEVE? 106
- DAY TWENTY-FIVE: NEW BEGINNING 112

STAGE VI: THE COVENANT 116
- DAY TWENTY-SIX: Be Still 117
- DAY TWENTY-SEVEN: ARE WE ONE BODY? 120
- DAY TWENTY-EIGHT: THE RIVER 123
- DAY TWENTY-NINE: THE RIVER...part II . 127
- DAY THIRTY: THE RAIN 131

STAGE VII: I AM HERE 135
- DAY THIRTY-ONE: ALIVE WITH CHRIST . 137
- DAY THIRTY-TWO: STAY HUMBLE 140
- DAY THIRTY-THREE: WHY, GOD? 142

DAY THIRTY-FOUR: ACTION VS. WORDS 148

DAY THIRTY-FIVE: BEWARE OF THE PUFFERFISH 153

STAGE VIII: SIDE WITH PEACE 161

DAY THIRTY-SIX: ALL THAT GLITTERS IS NOT GOLD 163

DAY THIRTY-SEVEN: THE ADVOCATE 173

DAY THIRTY-EIGHT: LOVE THY NEIGHBOR 175

DAY THIRTY-NINE: THE REFUGEE 178

DAY FORTY: SANCTUARY 180

EPILOGUE 183

THE ENTRANCE EXAM 185

ACKNOWLEDGEMENTS 187

PROLOGUE

The Israelites were God's chosen people. Through the covenant He made with Abraham, God promised that He would not let His people stay in bondage. He promised that He would bring justice to those who enslaved them.
Abram's offspring would come out with great possessions with the 4th generations returning back to the land that was promised them.

When the time was right, God sent Moses to lead the people from the House of Pharaoh. During their journey, to the promised land, God began to prepare the children of Israel for their new life. Many lessons were given to The Chosen People so they would start to learn to identify with WHO THEY WERE and HOW TO LIVE in covenant with God. One of those lessons came in the form of FRESH MANNA.

In the wilderness, the people complained of hunger. They needed to be fed, or they felt they would die. The Lord told Moses that He would rain bread from heaven each day for the people, but they had specific instructions to follow. God would also test them on whether or not they would adhere to His teachings.

FRESH MANNA was provided each morning as the dew lifted. For forty years, the Israelites ate FRESH MANNA until they came to the border of the Land of Canaan.

This meditation journal will take you on a journey over the next 40 days as you begin to rediscover yourself and see the world through the eyes of The Creator.

Spend each day in the devotions and reflecting upon the study questions. Take time to journal and spend in prayer. This is your intimate journey with God as He leads you to a New Beginning with Him.

Enjoy the Journey...

John 6:35 (NRSV) And Jesus said unto them, I am the bread of life: he that cometh to me shall never hunger; and he that believeth on me shall never thirst.
Exodus 16:35 (NRSV) When the Israelites saw it, they said to one another, "What is it?" For they did not know what it was. Moses said to them, "It is the bread that the LORD has given you to eat

MORE THAN JUST SOMEONE'S CHILD

The discussion of identity has been a substantial topic as of late. It seems apparent that it is essential to our Father that we know and understand who we are in Him.

Recently the conversation about the identity of our children and their roles and the responsibilities of parents have come to the forefront.

Today is my son's 21st birthday, and as I woke up and started my day, I felt God pressing me to rehash a previous discussion here with you, my friends.

I actually had this conversation (in some ways) with my now adult son on the eve of us traveling home, to spend with family, for his birthday.

It is interesting how people think about their lives and what they want, more specifically, the desire to have a family.

You hear people talk about the children they want and all the things they would want to do with them/show them.

When a woman becomes pregnant, many times there is much celebration of the new life that she is now carrying. The parents may be "showered" with gifts, some being supplies to help with the expenses of having a newborn. Parents (and sometimes, other family members) discuss/debate over baby names. Sometimes, unfortunately, additional factors may

arise causing anxiety or stress.
Such a precious gift we are given when we have the opportunity to bring a life into this world. Such a busy time of preparation as well.

In the midst of the excitement and business, when did the parent go to the TRUE CREATOR to obtain the identity of the life they were Blessed enough to bring into this world?

It is terrific to have thoughts about what WE want to share with our children, but I wonder if so many of the later arguments and disappointments were self-inflicted?

Have we, inadvertently, tried to control our children based on what WE 'UNDERSTOOD" would be best because of things we just read, heard, or experienced ourselves? Have we unintentionally began making mini-mes? We want so much to have someone to carry on our identity/legacy but who are these children really? When God gave them to you, who did HE say they were and were to become?

WAIT!!

Did you ever ask?

I am sure that we thanked Him for these "bundles of joy." BUT, gratitude for the Blessing of becoming a parent is more significant than feeling the excitement and thanking God.

Gratitude also comes in the form of receiving the proper instructions/directions to care for the gift received, THEN following those directions.

These little ones, as we already know, have a purpose and destiny and identity that goes far beyond just being our children.

Yes, we want them to be the best person they can be but what about being the best that God wants them to be?

We need to take a good look at our children and see them through the eyes of God, their Creator. We must realize that these children are our gifts given by God. These children, TRULY belong to HIM.

I Samuel I-
Hannah, a barren woman, wanted a child, prayed to God to Bless her to have the ability to have a child. In her prayers, she also told The Lord that if a child were given to her, she would return the child to God. Now, some would look at this as "bargaining" with God, but it goes to something more significant. Hannah understood that should God answer this prayer, she knew that this child, whom she would love, comes from the One she loved and honored. When Samuel was born, Hannah did precisely what she told God she would do. She gave this son to serve The Lord.
As Samuel studied under Eli, Hannah continued to make her son an Ephod (a sacred garment that is worn by high priests) every year.

This is important to take note of as it was more than Hannah just giving her son an annual gift. This gift she presented to Samuel was more of an investment in support of who he was becoming and who God would call him to be. Even ensuring Samuel had the "right" people in his life assured that he would grow in the direction God was calling for him. She set the foundation making room for Samuel to continue to grow into a fuller realization of God's purpose for his life.

Samuel, a seer, and a great leader became the man who God would use during one of the darkest hours of Israel's life. Even the name his mother gave him had meaning. It was not just a random name that she decided that she heard and liked (or thought it sounded nice). His name- God has heard was given to him because Hannah recognized that Samuel was the answer God gave to her prayers.

What have you named your children and why? What does his/her name mean? What does this name say about them or speak to who they are or will become? Have you checked the meaning of his/her name?

What gifts do you buy/give to your children? Are these gifts that will impact or invest in who they are or will become? Or are you providing gifts based on what you like or do not like or you think is the latest hot thing he/she will enjoy (for the moment)?

Have you REALLY observed your child to see the interests they take? OR are they developing interests solely based on your likes/wishes/wants/desires OR because "everyone else is interested?" Have you spent time investing in your child based on the life you WISHED you could have had or the life they are destined to have?

Let's HONOR God and give thanks for these wonderful

gifts He has given us by returning our children back to HIM. Let's do more than raise them based on our understanding…seeing so much of ourselves in them. Let's SEE them for who God created them to be/become. As they grow, see what God is doing and leading them towards. Let's take the time and do more than pray that they are safe and secure. Let's SEEK God and ask, "Who have You given me to raise, protect, love, and cherish?" When it is time to give to our children, let's ask "What will help to develop them to become who You are forming them to become?" Let's dig deeper before giving a name to God's precious children. After all, they will become heirs to His Kingdom. And THEN, let's be obedient and Trust the guidance we have been given, not leaning on our own understanding.

We MUST do EVERYTHING possible to ensure we are raising these children according to the standards set by The Creator. These lives we are responsible for are MORE than just our offspring…They belong to GOD and were designed with a purpose in mind.

This is dedicated to my beloved son whom I am so proud of. I thank God that He has allowed me to raise you. I am grateful that throughout the years, He has answered my prayers to let me see you through His eyes. God had provided, in many ways that I could never do on my own, so that you could become the person that He created you to be. Every instrument you desire/desired to learn to play, He made it possible for that to happen. Every science experiment you started in my freezer, He helped me to understand and support. Every idea you had about animals, God helped me see who He is was forming you to be. Now, as you will soon start your final year of undergrad and then move on to Grad school to become a Vet, I continue to remember the promise God has given me about you. I know with all of my heart that you will continue to do great things. You will accomplish things that one could only imagine, but if you continue to TRUST Him as well, He will take you far beyond what the human mind can comprehend.

Happy Birthday, Son! Love Mom

Fresh Manna: Journey To A New Beginning

STAGE I: EVERYTHING YOU EVER NEED

As you walk through the Meadows towards the forest, the path becomes dim as the trees begin to block the rays of the sun.
But there is a tree that stands firm and taller than all the other trees.

Look up and see how high this tree stands and full of life as you glance at the vibrant limbs and the fullness thereof.

This tree provides you shelter from the rain.

Its thick and firm trunk provides you a place to rest against when you are tired and weary.

Its fruit provides you nourishment when you are hungry and need strength to endure the rest of your walk.

The leaves provide you shelter and warmth when you are cold.

And should you dare to climb to reach the heart of the tree, the limbs/branches will provide a way up to lift you higher and higher.

As you continue to climb and dare to reach the top, you will see that the way ahead becomes clearer and more transparent.

Because, this tree, the tree of life, standing strong

Fresh Manna: Journey To A New Beginning

above everything else, has provided all you need for the journey ahead.

Fresh Manna: Journey To A New Beginning

DAY ONE: TRUST GOD

Today as with many other days, I set out on a morning hike. I usually go hiking as a form of exercise as well as meditation. I noticed that shortly after I began hiking back in November, God would start speaking to me about many different things and people. Many times the hike would turn out to be a lesson that I would see as shown by Him.

This particular day, I knew I needed to clear my thoughts mainly from a set of events that occurred this past weekend. I had a meeting this evening and wanted to ensure I went in with a clear mind, therefore, allowing the Holy Spirit to be my guide during the conference. What I was not expecting was to come off the trail with a new assignment and challenge from God.

Today, He said, he gave me a set number of days to walk with Him as He would continue to pour out fresh revelation to me. I would begin to see even more than before, and I was to write the lesson of the day. This journey would be the second book I would publish this year. Keep in mind that I was just beginning the first and wondered how all this would be accomplished, after all, I was also in seminary school. Of course, the first day, the lesson would be about trust.

I set out on a familiar trail I had not only completed previously with a small guided group, but I had done this same one alone a couple of times. Today was different. For starters, as I began, I felt a little different. I wondered if I would remember my way through. Why has this thought even come over me? I

Fresh Manna: Journey To A New Beginning

know I have been away for about two weeks on vacation, but it's not like this is a challenging trail to follow. It is basically a loop, at the lower end of the Estrella Mountains, just shy of five miles.

I began at the usual starting point, donned on my camelback and my headphones, started my music and my hiking map app. Soon after, I saw the sign for the trail I knew I had to eventually begin on but knew the direction it was pointing was not the way I had gone before. When shown the way initially, we went straight but caught the end of the trail around this particular point. I keep going. As I am moving, I get warmed up, take off my hoodie, tied it around my waist and continued to move forward. Next thing I knew, I suddenly got a burst of energy. I have not been out running for quite some time, but at this moment, I felt like I could run part of this particular hike. I set out slowly attacking each climb that came. First taking small steps then with this jolt of energy, I began running up each slope or hill. As I reached each one, I felt stronger and stronger and moving up each slope with longer strides. Eventually, I found myself running on the flat ground way before the hill. I feel good. I got this! Now, I am doing intervals. I can run a minute and walk pretty fast the next. I continued this until I reached a crossroad.

Standing at this crossroad, the road ahead looked unfamiliar. How is that? I have been here time and time again. I am pretty confident I must keep going straight but why am I thinking to go left? This cannot be right. I reach for my phone to pull up the route saved under my previous hikes. The phone is moving but extremely slow considering I have a pretty good signal. I try to use another application to pull up the route, and I cannot get it to come up. I can see the name of the route but cannot get the actual map or directions to load. Interesting, as my music is playing, and so is the tracker I have running on the phone. I give in and go left, but I am sauntering because this just seems off. I keep moving anyway. The road looks different. I know the name of this part of the trail, but this is not the part I have been guided on previously.

As I look up and forward, I see the back of barrier signs. Strange…now I know this is not right but I hear, keep going. I get to the end of this road which was about a quarter of a mile, and it is really the end of the road. You can step across the little divider that marks the end of the trail but on the other side is just a parking lot. An empty parking lot. This is the beginning of this particular trail, not the continuation of mine. I have to head back and get on the right path for me, so I do just that…double back and go the direction I initially questioned.

As I continue, I notice again, new uphill climbs but I can take them on with no problems. Yet, for some reason, I periodically look back just confirming I am in the right place and going in the right direction. Hey, I can always turn around and go back, right? No, there is no way, I am going back. I have to be on the trail that is leading me in the right direction. It did just that. I got to the next crossroad and there it was, the path I knew I eventually needed to get to. It was there all along. Why did I doubt so much?

This is what God showed me.

He said, we so often ask, "Lord, show me the way in which I should go." He shows us and when it is time to walk that particular path this is what we do:

We may start off slow only for a moment, and as it seems right, we just keep moving as long as we can see the road ahead. Even when obstacles come, we wonder if we can get through but with His help we do. This only somewhat increases our faith, just enough to climb over more obstacles on the road we can see. When we get to a crossroad, despite the fact He has already shown us the way to go, we stop, question, doubt and even try to figure things out on our own. The problem with that is that you end up in unfamiliar territory. A place that was not meant for you but maybe for someone else. Their road looks different than yours, but you tried to make it work for you. When you realize that it doesn't and leads you to an unwanted end, you ask again for help. Help to get out and back to where you were supposed to be. Because of His grace and mercy, He sets you back and shows you again, the direction you must go. As we move, we look back wondering, this cannot be right. God said, where is your trust?

He says, "For I am the same God that kept His promise to deliver the children of Israel from bondage." He is a God that keeps His promises but failing to trust Him brings us problems. In Genesis 46:3-4, God told Jacob to fear not to go down into Egypt; for He would make thee a great nation there. He did not let Jacob go alone, in fact, He even said that He would go WITH him. If God told you and showed you where to go and is with you all the way, why do we need to try and stop to figure things out on our own?

TRUST GOD. He will never leave you nor forsake you.

Readings: Genesis 46:3-4; Psalms 9:10

Reflections:

1. What have you been seeking God for?
2. How long have you been working to get to where God needs to take you?
3. Are you one the right path? What do you need to change?
4. How can you begin to trust God more to guide you rather than leaning on your own understanding or way?
5. Why have you been afraid to Trust God fully and completely? Who are you listening to?

DAY TWO: TAKE A STAND
God has not called you to FIT IN

A small group of us met to take our weekly morning hike. Geared up and ready to go, I head to the park to meet with the others. The trail was decided, and we met at the trail entry point. I heard the trail we would take but thinking, I only know of part of this trail. I am unsure that I have been on the back end of it, where it actually ends. Good thing we have a ranger and volunteers to lead.

We meet at the designated place and ensure everyone is ready to move out. Our leader is right in front guiding us along. There are routine stops along the way for water and rest. At one point, we stop, and I hear my name...Shawanda, have you met "T"? No, I replied. Oh, well let me introduce you. I think I have no idea what I am in for, but it must be impressive because the others in the group are chuckling.

Since this was my first time on this trail with the group, the leader wanted to ensure I knew all of the relevant details, even the cactus that was named after a former hiker. She told the story of this person in detail. How she was part of the group and moved away, her intriguing story of love and sacrifice for her nieces and nephews, as she had no children. Apparently, this person would come out to all the events that families would attend with children. During these events, they would give away tickets to a particular water park. Not having children of her own, she came alone but with a purpose. To hopefully win passes for her nieces and nephews and one day, it all paid off, she won. Everyone in the group laughed as they remembered this lovely person and talked about how much she must have loved her nieces and nephews. What a great aunt, someone said.

To think, this woman, showed up to events alone that others came with children. Daring to stand out from the crowd, all to obtain what she was seeking. After doing this for some time, towards the end, it all paid off. The very thing she wanted she received and to top it all off, it really was never about her. What she wanted, she knew would bring joy to others. She showed sacrifice and dedication. How many of us would have done the same thing? Would we be too concerned with how others would look at us? What might they say about us? Or would we have the gall to step out alone and do something different all, for the cause?

God had me think if you believe in something, are you courageous enough to step out or stand up, even if others do not? If you believe in ME, He says, will you take a stand or sit down and fade into the background? Are you bold enough to proclaim my name even if others do not? Are you willing to speak on what is right, even if it makes you stand out or will you go along with others or what they may think and back down from your convictions? What are you willing to sacrifice for ME? Is your reputation more significant than the reward of a place in My Kingdom? What about your pride? Is that more important to you?

Romans 12:1-3 (NRSV), Tells us to present ourselves as a living sacrifice, holy, acceptable unto God, which is our reasonable service. We are not to be conformed to this world but transformed by the renewing of our mind that we may prove what is that good, and acceptable, perfect will of God.

We are not to think too highly of ourselves but know that our true identity is in Christ. When faced with a situation you become weary of making a sacrifice and standing out, remember the ultimate sacrifice that was made for you...Christ was the sacrificial lamb. Crucified so that you may live. Such a great gift was given to you by the sacrifice and Love of our Lord and Savior. Do not forget, He too was persecuted by those that did not believe Him or believe in Him.

Although many will see you as strange and you feel persecuted on earth for what you believe, greater is thy reward in heaven for "the first shall be last, and the last shall be first." (Matthew 19:30) Be willing to accept social disapproval knowing that you have God's approval for eternal reward is higher than the temporary earthly reward.

Readings: Romans 12:1-3, Matthew 19:30, I Peter 2:5

Reflections:

1. Are you courageous to believe in something despite what others may say or believe?
2. Are you willing to believe in what God has promised you, even others do not?
3. How will you continue to proclaim the promise when other will not?
4. Will you stand, believing in God or are you more concerned with what everyone else thinks or believes?
5. Are you part of the pack or leading it?

DAY THREE: SHED and SURRENDER

So many times we get frustrated because it seems like we are in a place where things are not moving the way we want them to. It looks like the people we need to hear us are not listening, no one quite understands what you are going through, but you are desperately seeking some sort of resolve.

These are times when you have to understand that you are actually in a place where you may need to "shed." See, what's happening is that you are stuck yourself. It seems like no one understands because you refuse to see things from a side other than yours. You are looking for an answer that will satisfy you (and your flesh) rather than accepting the answer that will bring you true resolve. This is the answer that may make you take a hard look at what you need to change. You may need to change your thought process, you may need to change your surroundings, things in your lifestyle, etc. Unfortunately, we do not like change, and more importantly, we do not like real accountability, we just like satisfaction.

It's like when we go to God in prayer asking for so much, but yet we turn around and say, He is not answering my prayers, Why must I continue to struggle? Well, you are struggling because you want to do things your way. You want to hear what you want to hear. You want something that will satisfy your flesh. You want God's response to align up with your request rather than surrendering to what His will is. So now, this struggle you are having is genuinely you fighting against what God has and wants for you. It is the unnecessary struggle. It is the fight against your

destiny, the fight against your freedom, the fight against your peace.

Rather than putting up the unnecessary fight, "shed." Shed yourself and surrender. Sit and hear the direction God has for you. Sit and hear what He wants you to do. Yes, you may need to do things that may seem "uncomfortable" to you, but it is for your good. You may need to have some "uncomfortable" conversations, but it is for your good. You may have to shed some tears, but it is cleansing for the soul. Will there be some challenges along the way on your journey towards your destiny? Absolutely, but at least you will have His covering rather than trying to fight against Him while you are on your own and being disobedient. At least with Him, you will have Peace, Freedom, and Victory.

Reflections:

1. What are you struggling with?
2. What situation in your life seems to keep repeating?
3. Ask God, Is this the plan? Listen to God.
4. What are the flaws in your plan?
5. What actions or thoughts do you need to change to align yourself with God's plan? (This will continue to evolve during the journey)

DAY FOUR: THE LIGHT WITHIN
"Your light will shine when all else fades."

STAR IS RISING...

Not one embellished with lavish things but one who shines brightly and lights up the world around them.

Rise up...Shine and be that guiding light

Those lost can look up to and see this star shining brightly, leading them out of the wilderness, the desert, and dark places

SHINE BRIGHT STAR, SHINE

It is not about all the worldly things in life that make you shine. For one could have fancy cars, clothes, and all the money in the world, yet still be rotten in the core...their heart and soul.

So, today, I ask you, What is in your heart? What makes you shine?

My grandmother used to sing this song, This Little Light of Mine. I can still hear her voice singing,

"This little light of mine, I'm gonna let it shine, let shine, let it shine, let it shine..."

It was a catchy tune, but one day, she gave it more meaning to me. As she dropped me off at a friend's house, she said, "Let your light shine."

Jesus said, "You are the

light of the world. A city built on a hill cannot be hid. No one after lighting a lamp puts it under the bushel basket, but on the lampstand, and it gives light to all in the house. In the same way, let your light shine before others, so that they may see your good works and give glory to your Father in heaven" (Matthew 5:14-16, NRSV)

To put it in the purest form, it is what you do that makes you shine and will last. It is not about the flashy possessions you chase after that gives you "bling" (as this generation says).

So, the next time you see others that seem to have such a great life because of their wealth and flashy attire, fret not. Do not compare and wish you had what they had. For there is nothing wrong with wealth but that is not what makes you SHINE.

Readings: Matthew 5:14-16

Reflections:

1. When you look in the mirror, who do you see? What do you see or take notice of immediately?
2. How do others see you? What is the first thing they notice? The things you have or do not have or the radiant glow you exuberate?
3. A heart and soul that smiles can light up a room and bring comfort and warmth to others. Is this something you radiate or do you/have you expected your outer appearance to make the entrance for you?
4. How can you let the light within you shine greater and brighter for all to see?

DAY FIVE: ANCHORS

There are two ways an anchor can be used in your life:

There is the anchor that keeps you from drifting away, especially in times of storm.

Then there is the anchor that holds you down (or back) and keeps you from sailing

Sometimes, we have people in our lives that are like the anchor that holds you still, preventing you from moving. This anchor keeps you from sailing and exploring what life has for you. It keeps you from seeing what is out there for you to conquer. This anchor becomes cumbersome and a dead weight, causing you just to drag along.

"When daylight came, they did not recognize the land, but they saw a bay with a sandy beach, where they decided to run the ship aground if they could. Cutting loose the anchors, they left them in the sea and at the same time untied the ropes that held the rudders. Then they hoisted the foresail to the wind and made for the beach" (Acts 27:39-40, *NIV*).

Listen, when you get tired of sitting in the storm and not moving, throw that dead weight overboard. Stop trying to pull everyone along with you. Sometimes, you have to cut the ropes and leave them behind while you set sail for greater things…new heights.

The best anchor you could ever have is Jesus. For He

will keep you even when the storms come. God will not let you just drift aimlessly. When it's time to move, He is not a weight to hold you down nor hold you back. NO, He is THE ONE you can ANCHOR your hopes in as you move and progress.

So, the questions today are:

What anchors are in your life?

Is your anchor a helper or hindrance?

Readings: Acts 27:39-40

Reflections:

1. When you look in the mirror, who do you see? What do you see or take notice of immediately?
2. How do others see you? What is the first thing they notice? The things you have or do not have or the radiant glow you exuberate?
3. A heart and soul that smiles can light up a room and bring comfort and warmth to others. Is this something you radiate or do you/have you expected your outer appearance to make the entrance for you?
4. How can you let the light within you shine greater and brighter for all to see?

STAGE II: WALK WITH ME

The LORD God is my strength, and he will make my feet like hind's feet, and He will make me to walk upon high places..."

It was dark, but you continued to walk with Me, through the woods, can you see the break of day through the trees?

Brighter...Clearer...do you see?

Look closer as you began to come through and out. The way is clearing.

The trees are not as close.

Look up as you come through the clearance

The mist clears as the hills begin to ascend.

The peaks are beginning to come into focus yet in a small but great cloud.

KEEP WALKING...DO NOT STOP...YOU CANNOT TURN BACK NOW

ACROSS THE FIELD AND TOWARDS THE MOUNTAINTOP YOU MUST GO

DAY SIX: JUST A LITTLE FAITH

"Meanwhile, the disciples were in trouble far away from land, for a strong wind had risen, and they were fighting heavy waves. About three o'clock in the morning Jesus came toward them, walking on the water. When the disciples saw him walking on the water, they were terrified. In their fear, they cried out, 'It's a ghost.' But Jesus spoke to them at once. 'Don't be afraid,' he said. 'Take courage. I am here!' Then Peter called to him, 'Lord, if it's really you, tell me to come to you, walking on the water.' 'Yes, come,' Jesus said. So Peter went over the side of the boat and walked on the water toward Jesus. But when he saw the strong wind and the waves, he was terrified and began to sink. 'Save me, Lord!' he shouted. Jesus immediately reached out and grabbed him. 'You have so little faith,' Jesus said. 'Why did you doubt me?'" (Matthew 14:24-31, *NLT*)

TODAY...

Get out of the boat and keep your eye on Jesus. For Peter looked away, afraid of what was happening around him, although Jesus was right in front of him.

So many times the disciples saw Jesus perform signs and wonders, as they walked with Him, yet, they seemed to question often what they saw.

Fresh Manna: Journey To A New Beginning

They watched Him feed the multitude with five loaves of bread and two fish, still amazed. They watched Him heal the sick, give sight to the blind, and even cast out demons, yet shocked.

How much do you need to see before you believe?

How many times must He save you before you believe?

How much must He provide before you believe?

If only you had FAITH...Even the size of a mustard seed.

A mustard seed is such a tiny seed, but as it grows, it becomes such an enormous tree.

So much comes from something so tiny.

Today, I encourage you to have faith in Christ Jesus. Even if your faith is the size of a tiny mustard seed. For if you start there, it will continue to grow like that of the tree that came from that seed.

Faith healed the woman with the issue of blood (Mark 5:34)

Faith healed Bartimaeus, once blind now given sight (Mark 10:52)

What have you been asking God for but have been lacking in faith?

What will your faith do?

Fresh Manna: Journey To A New Beginning

Readings: Matthew 14:24-31 , Mark 5:34, Mark 10:52

Reflections:

1. What have you been asking God for? Have you stopped believing that it can come true?
2. Even in the darkest hour are you still able to hold on to your faith to see the light of day? Is your faith failing or prevailing?

DAY SEVEN: POSITIONING YOURSELF FOR BATTLE

We often hear or quote the scripture that the battle is not yours (ours) but the Lord's (God's), but we also forget that while God is fighting, there are instructions He gives us to follow. What should we do while He is fighting on our behalf?

II Chronicles 20:1-30

When Jehoshaphat heard that a great multitude was coming against him (and his people) from Edom, he was afraid and sought the Lord and proclaimed a fast throughout Judah. He recognized the power and faithfulness of God and cried out for His help, knowing that God would hear the cries of His people and save them.

As all the people stood before the Lord, His spirit fell upon Jahaziel, and He spoke:

"Don't be afraid or discouraged by this great army because the battle isn't yours. It belongs to God! 16 March out against them tomorrow. Since they will be coming through the Ziz pass, meet them at the end of the valley that opens into the Jeruel wilderness. 17 You don't need to fight this battle. Just take your places, stand ready, and watch how the Lord, who is with you, will deliver you, Judah and Jerusalem. Don't be afraid or discouraged! Go out tomorrow and face them. The Lord will be with you."

Now, this is where most of us leave the story and carry on, but we do not note an important fact here.

They were never told to do nothing. In fact, there were things they actually had to do. Many times, we say "This is The Lord's Battle" without realizing that we also have a position that we are required to take as well.

Look at the critical instructions they were given:

1. Tomorrow march out against them
2. Meet them at the end of the valley that opens into the Jeruel wilderness
3. Take your places, stand ready and watch how the Lord is with you and will deliver you
4. Don't be afraid or discouraged
5. GO out tomorrow and face them

They did not just sit back or turn away hoping and wishing the Lord would take up everything. No, they went and positioned themselves for a battle already won.

That morning they rose and went out but BELIEVING in The Lord. Furthermore, they went forth with those who would sing to the Lord and Praise Him in holy splendor BEFORE the army.

As they sang and praised The Lord, He launched the attack destroying all of the enemy's armies. When Judah arrived, all they saw were corpses on the ground. What was left was all the blessings (riches of the fallen), more than they could carry that it took three days to haul away.

God said, I will fight, BUT you MUST take up YOUR

Fresh Manna: Journey To A New Beginning

position for battle

POSITION OF FAITH...

POSITION OF OBEDIENCE...

POSITION OF PRAISE

AND THEN He will move, and you shall reap the rewards.

Readings: II Chronicles 20:1-30

Reflections:

1. While you are waiting/expecting The Lord to do great things, what are you doing in the meantime?
2. Are you constantly sulking when adversity comes your way or do you recover from your emotions knowing that God is yet still at work? Therefore, you can praise Him in advance for the victory?
3. How can you position yourself for Battle?

DAY EIGHT: CHAMPION

In every season we get ready to watch our favorite sports teams throw down on the field, court, etc. In preparation, we've studied up on all the previous season's stats, watched the drafts, put in our opinions about who should play for what teams, and dusted off our favorite jerseys to put on to show our allegiance to our teams. Then we spend countless hours watching them, cheering them on, and talking trash about their opponents. But, don't you know that there are seasons in which God also works in our lives and the lives of others?

What if we spent as much time recognizing how God is moving in each season, as we spend seeing how our favorite teams will advance in each season?

For in this season, God wants to open doors for you. In this season, He wants to connect you to the right circle of people who will help you move in the direction that you have been dreaming and praying about. In this coming season, He says, I am ready to pour out my blessings upon you, but you must prepare for the season.

It's time to dust off the old "playbook." The book you wrote down all of your goals, desires, and dreams. It's time to get back to work and refocus on the road ahead. For a while, you are sitting back preparing to invest all of your time and effort in watching those who are achieving or have achieved their goals, your lack of work will keep you from meeting yours. Your lack of focus and energy will only allow someone else get ahead while you just wish and dream.

Fresh Manna: Journey To A New Beginning

Don't get passed by this season...

Rather than focusing on putting on your favorite team's jersey/colors, put on your own colors. Give yourself a push. Cheer yourself on. Study to get yourself ahead. Surround yourself with a team that will push and motivate you.

In this season, strive to be...THE CHAMPION

Reflections:

1. We all want the promise but are you prepared to receive it?
2. What preparations have you made to succeed in what God has planned for you?
3. What is your strategy for success and continued success?
4. How will you handle setbacks and roadblocks?
5. What "tools" are you gathering to fill your "toolbox"?

DAY NINE: THE GATHERING

As you look at history and study traditions, one of the oldest traditions is that of storytelling. Within several cultures, it was customary for people to gather together to tell, hear, and/or share stories that were passed down through the generations.

Some of these stories would tell of the lives of people/ancestors bringing things like encouragement and hope to those listening. Some stories would just give life lessons and could allow the listeners to relate and maybe find their purpose in life. These stories are lessons of things like love, hope, joy, obedience, courage, strength, faith, promise, perseverance, integrity, and freedom.

You see these same gatherings throughout the Bible. They are revealed in understanding the customs of those gathering to be taught lessons or meeting to hear, read, and learn the scriptures. You can know that stories of the ancestors were shared. Ancestors like:

- Abraham - who was willing to sacrifice a great gift, still knowing and holding onto the promise still yet to come

OR

- Moses - who would stand in the face of his enemy, commanding that his people were freed and rising up to become a leader of his people.

Even now, people gather and tell stories of ancestors. Though time has changed the concept of gathering may vary but what does not or has not changed are the types of stories or lessons shared. Maybe even there are new stories with new characters.

As time changes and these traditions continue, your story will also be told and passed down BUT what will they gather to hear about you?

Will we gather to learn that you:

- had courage like David? He stood up to defeat Goliath with way less than any soldier was equipped with. Who was also humble enough to know that he was anointed king by God through the prophet Samuel, yet understood how to follow and serve the king still seated on the throne until it was his appointed time to be seated and placed in position.

- Had the faith and trust of Noah? He was not an architect but trusted what God put in him to build an ark that was 300 cubits in length, 50 cubits wide, and 30 cubits high (450x75x45 ft) equal to 1 ½ football fields in length

- Were like apostle Paul? After an encounter with Christ, he would be forever changed. He would now see the world with new vision and make it his life's mission to spread how he was transformed and lead others to a life of transformation facing persecution but standing firm in his faith. His demonstration of faith, obedience, boldness, and leadership became an example for others to follow.

- Had faith like the woman with the issue of blood? She knew what she needed (to get healed) and gave everything she had in her to make her way, pushing her way through the crowds to get to that source (Jesus).

- Were like Jeremiah? He thought he was too young to go and do the great things God asked, overcame that by believing who God said he was, going on to speak in front of rulers.

OR

Will we gather to hear that you were more like:

- Cain - lacking wisdom, understanding, and accountability? Stuck in his own jealousy, he failed to understand why his brother, Abel's offering was acceptable before God. While Cain provided an offering to God, Abel gave his first and best to God. Angry at God's favor to Abel, he not only killed his brother but when questioned by God, his response showed no accountability for his actions. His actions not only affected him but that of his ancestors. The blessings of the descendants of Adam and Eve would now begin with the birth of their son, Seth.

- King Saul- the first appointed king. Later, feared man and followed them rather than the instructions of God, had the kingdom ripped from him, and lost the favor of God.

Stories to reflect upon...but what will your story be? What will they gather together and say about you?

Fresh Manna: Journey To A New Beginning

As you sit and reflect on your day, think:

If people gathered to tell my story, am I really living my best life? Am I revealing the best characteristics? Am I living a purposeful life or am I squandering away this precious gift?

What is my story?

What will they gather to hear of me?

I encourage you to make the steps to live your best life, taking advantage of opportunities presented you to, and having the courage to follow your dreams. If the idea to accomplish something or to be something great is in you, it is because God has put it there. C'mon...Make your story great! You've got this!

Reflections:

1. Who are you?
2. What is your story?
3. Would the story tell, match what others tell?
3. What must change for the stories to align?
4. Are you taking every opportunity to make your story great? How?

DAY TEN: WHO HAS YOUR IDENTITY

On one side of the fence, you have those who are captivated by audiences doing things to be seen. Hoping others will see what you claim to be the *real you*. This *real you* is not even the *real you* that you need to learn to know.

The *real you* that you know is the one shining above all others. Loud and proud about who you are based on what we all see.

All along, the true you has been in need of much help. The true you covers up the emotional scars and baggage of this *real you* persona while walking around carefully and cautiously hoping not to be exposed.

"What will they think if I let them see the true me versus the *real me*? Will they think I am weak when I need them to see that I am strong? No, I cannot have the truth exposed. This can't happen. They will lose respect for me. I built something here with them, but it's based on the *real me*."

"The *real me* has been through way too much, but the true me is sometimes fearful that I can step back into my past. The true me cannot be carefree because the truth is, I have not truly healed. The true me has wounds that are still mending because I am stuck on why things happened to me, but I need everyone to see the battle scars of the real me. No one can know that healing is still required. No one can know that I haven't fully come to understand WHO I AM."

"I still suffer an identity crisis. Meanwhile, I have

compromised and allowed me to find my identity in those around me. See, if I only give them the persona of the *real me* then because they see me as strong, then I can identify as strong. When they see me as successful, then I identify as being successful. When I flaunt my "battle scars" then they call me victorious, so I identify as victorious. When they call me smart, I identify as the smart one."

"But, when I am alone when they are not around, then WHO AM I NOW?"

Well, ...that is the question of the hour.

The identity I have found in the "they" will only get me so far. It only lasts as long as "they" are present and actively around. I can't have a temporary or conditional identity. This identity only feeds my emotional state and gives me that "high" if I get to show it off in front of others. There has to be more to this identity thing than this emotional roller coaster. THIS IS NOT THE WAY TO LIVE!

Identity...WHO YOU ARE can only indeed come from THE ONE who created you. THE ONE who gave you life before anyone saw you in the flesh. THE ONE who made you in His image and after His likeness.

Jeremiah 1:4-5 Now the word of the LORD came to me saying, "Before I formed you in the womb I knew you, And before you were born I consecrated you; I have appointed you a prophet to the nations."

God knew you, just as He knew Jeremiah, long before you were born or conceived. He created you with a plan (or purpose) in mind, therefore, giving you an IDENTITY. God has always known how great you were. He LOVED you so much that He never wanted your identity hidden from you. Throughout your life, He has been showing you glimpses of WHO YOU REALLY ARE.

Do you think that you excelled in certain subjects, just to collect accolades and Attaboys from the world? NO! This was a scale being removed from your eyes. Letting you see a little of you through Him.

Remember the "odd" interests you had that others just didn't quite understand? They labeled you as "different" than others because you did not "fit in." You needed to see your uniqueness through His eyes.

Why were you created? You think it was just to be another number to add to the census report? NO! God created you with a purpose in mind.

It is time to start putting all the pieces of your life together to unveil the beautiful picture of YOU, as seen through the eyes of God, your Creator.

Psalms 139:13-16 (NRSV)
For you formed my inward parts;
you knitted me together in my mother's womb.
[14] I praise you, for I am fearfully and wonderfully made.
Wonderful are your works;
my soul knows it very well.
[15] My frame was not hidden from you,
when I was being made in secret,

> intricately woven in the depths of the earth.
> ¹⁶ Your eyes saw my unformed substance;
> in your book were written, every one of them,
> the days that were formed for me,
> when as yet there was none of them.

On the other side of the fence…there is the one who looks beyond the veil. There is the one who knows their true self as seen through the eyes of The Father.

On the other side of the fence…stands one who knows their true identity. Standing before "them" saying, "I will not be identified by the "they" for "they" do not dictate who I am. "They" did not give me purpose. "In fact, "they" may very well be the ones, I was created to help find their identity. Those life experiences I had, they were meant for me to share, to give them hope. To let them know that I found that those battles helped "mold" me into the person I am today. My scars are a testament to the strength I was given to endure, and I give God the glory because He never gave up on me, even when I wanted to give up. My scars are a testament that He always had something better planned for me. I no longer focus on the fact that so much has happened to me, I focus on the fact that, if that was all my life had to offer, I would not be standing today.

As I stop being so concerned about how others see my past, I can see my future. Not my future in "them" but my future in HIM.

Friends, I ask you, WHO ARE YOU? Take time to sit with Our Father and ask Him who you are. Remember, we were made in His image and likeness, He is not made in ours. This means that you will need to stop looking at yourself through the limited eyes of mankind. God's mind does not work like ours. Sometimes, we are limited by what we see in the natural, forgetting that Our Father does not sit in the flesh, so we have to open our minds to see through the eyes of The Spirit. There is so much greater than what is reflected in the natural eye.

I pray that God will speak to the eyes of your heart. That He gives you wisdom and understanding. That He gives you clarity to understand who He created you to be. That you walk in the fullness of the life that God has predestined for you. I pray that you find your true purpose in life, never seeking your identity through the limited eyes of mankind. I pray that as you discover the true you, you will never surrender again to the *"real you."*

May you grow in the things of God and be confident in WHO YOU ARE, never again to have an identity crisis.

BE BLESSED, BE BOLD, BELIEVE

Readings:
Jeremiah 1:4-5, Psalm 139-13-16

Reflections:

1. Who is the real you?
2. Is the real you and the true you the same?

3. What do you cover in public yet attempt to deal with in private?
4. Have you convinced yourself this is who you are or what you like because it works best in public or you have just go along with the status quo?
5. Have you created a new reality or identity based on what others say or believe things should be?
6. Do you really know what you want in or out of life?
7. Ask God who He says you are? Who He created you to be? How does He see you?

STAGE III: DESTINY AWAITS

Ridden With Guilt, Shame, Hurt, Anger

You Find Yourself First Exposed, Now Isolated

Scorn, Hopeless, Loathful

Looking For Answers To Every Problem You Didn't Realize You Had

Rise, young man, Rise like Dorcas from the dead

Death has surrounded you but should not overtake you

Greater is He that's in me than he that's in the world

See yourself in Me

Make Me your reflection

Let me give you new lenses

For I have given you purpose

Designed with a plan in mind

Step off the world's "merry go round" of life
It's had you spinning in circles way too long

Dizziness, sickness is all that has left you with

Fresh Manna: Journey To A New Beginning

Come drink of the Water

Let Me REFRESH you

Refreshing your foundation

Let Me restore what's rightfully yours

Overwhelmed and overtaken by fear

This is not a gift nor spirit I have given

For I have given you PEACE, LOVE, JOY, AND A SOUND MIND

For I AM the Bread of Life

Feed from Me, the love, hope, and sanctity

These are spirits that breathe LIFE

Perplexed and in the palms of your enemy

It's time to take a leap of faith

JUMP, JUMP, JUMP to your DESTINY

I shall reveal my plan to and for you

Designed with a purpose in mind

You are special My child

Fresh Manna: Journey To A New Beginning

Created out of love

Glorious days are ahead

But you must stop grasping at straws

Grasp my hand that will hold you...guide you and even push you

DESTINY AWAITS, PEACE AWAITS, JOY AWAITS...It's yours for the taking

My hand is strong, but My Love is stronger

DAY ELEVEN: SMALL BEGINNINGS

Do not despise the days of small beginnings. For God is pleased to see the work begin.

Think of a tiny seed that is planted. As it is nourished, it will begin to sprout up and continues to grow over time.

Now, replace that seed with the ideas and dreams that God has given you.

You may have started a book and thought, it's not selling very quickly or much.

You may have started a business, and your customer base is so small that it is tough to imagine it prospering as you desire.

What about the songs you've written and had only sung or played before a handful of people.

The art you've created and only your family and friends now appreciate...

The list could go on and on.

You cannot get discouraged and quit, thinking this is not how it's supposed to be.

Do you not realize the courage you had even to begin such a work? For this alone, you should be proud of yourself. It is not easy for everyone to take that first step in creating something and putting it out for exposure.

Fresh Manna: Journey To A New Beginning

God is pleased, for you have begun the work. You have laid a foundation that He can help you to continue to build upon.

Zerubbabel was the leader of the tribe of Judah when they returned from exile. He began rebuilding the temple that was built by King Solomon and destroyed by the Babylonians.

This new temple took two years just to build the foundation. After "celebrating" the success of the beginning of the building, opposition soon followed. The people were discouraged and made afraid to build. The opposition even bribed officials to frustrate their plan.

This happens when you have finally moved on your plan. You're excited and cannot wait to keep moving along for you know that success is present and will continue.

Then comes those who try to trample on your hopes and dreams. They compare your results to their expectations...shooting down your "small beginnings."

Now, you are discouraged. You went from seeing the great work you started to now believing it's too small to make a difference. This is all understandable. Afterall, the people who returned from exile and worked so hard to build the temple, they too had been discouraged, harassed by their enemies, and tired but they had something greater. The people had God on their side...YOU, HAVE GOD ON YOUR SIDE.

Did this temple have the same splendor as the

original? No, it was actually built on a smaller scale, BUT it had a GREATER Glory. This would be the temple in which THE MESSIAH would come and walk the grounds.

What you have now may not look like much. It may not look like what others think it should. Just keep building...brick by brick...keep building...when opposition comes, don't worry because what God has given you to do, NO OPPOSITION can stop.

Be faithful in small opportunities. BEGIN where you are, do what you can, and LEAVE THE RESULTS TO GOD

Readings: Ezra 4-6, Zechariah 4:8-10

Reflections:

1. Have you thought about starting something new?
2. Have you begun something yet results are not as great as you expected?
3. Why do you think God started you on this path? What was He trying to show you?
4. Think about things you have accomplished. Now reflect upon the impact made. Have you done more than you have given yourself credit for?
5. How do you measure accomplishment/success?

DAY TWELVE: NEW VISION

Through what lenses do you view the world...with what vision do you see others...with what vision do you see life?

Do you look through the lenses of murky colored waters? Do you have distorted or blurry vision?

Do you see all that is wrong with everything or can you find any glimpse of love or peace?

Life is not supposed to be simple...never seeing or experiencing/encountering the hands/works of the evil one but have you allowed those weeds to strangle your life?

Do you now see everything through the eyes of pain or sorrow?

When I was on active duty, we would say that perception is reality.

What you perceive to be real then becomes real (to you).

If you are looking through water colored lenses, then your view is always distorted...unclear...murky

Let's look at the world around us.

Throughout history, yes, you will find many events that upset or cause you grief...they were unpleasant times.

In your life, there are many of these similar events ...events that cause: pain, sorrow, grief, despair, darkness, and failure.

BUT will this cause you to see the rest of your world...your life the same way?

Someone hurts you, and now the perception is that many are like this. So, you withdraw...your vision has been distorted.

This hurt is like dirt on the lenses of your glasses.

The times of sorrow...more dirt

Every unthinkable act or thing in your life...more dirt

With all the dirt on your lenses, no wonder you cannot see clearly. All you can see is dirt.

The great thing about dirt is that it can be removed...you just need a cleaning agent

Mark 8:22-26, Jesus restores sight to a blind man in Bethsaida, but it did not happen all at once. This miracle was a two-stage process. The first time Jesus touch him, the man looked up and said that he saw men as trees walking. Unable to see at all at first, his sight is now BEING restored. The second time Jesus touched him, he was restored.

Mark 10:46-52, A blind beggar, Bartimaeus, made a decision to call {cry} out to Jesus for help. He had never seen the miracles performed by Jesus, but he had heard of them. With just what he heard, he had enough faith to cry out for help from Jesus for himself. He understood who Jesus was, The Messiah {son of David}, and not just what Jesus could do for him.

Why are these two stories important?

- You need your vision restored, you need to BELIEVE and CRY out to Jesus for help just like Bartimaeus. For God is a healer and deliverer. He can restore all of which was once lost.
- Even as you are healed and delivered from the things of your past, it is a process for the full restoration of your vision. That first touch may clear somethings up, BUT you will need to stay in the presence of God for your complete healing.

Let me put this in a more personable context:

I can relate to the hurt, pains, and sorrows of life. Having gone through situations that at one point, all I could think of was WHY ME? My vision was getting murky. Things some spoke into my life, was like throwing more dirt on my already dirty lenses. Like Bartimaeus, I had not seen the actual works of Jesus, but I had heard of them so I too, cried out to Him for help. Whatever He put on the inside of me, that I really did not even understand then, made me fail to see myself as a victim. As I continued to encounter people who tried to further dirty my lenses, I believed that My God was bringing me through.

Fresh Manna: Journey To A New Beginning

The more tribulations I have encountered throughout my life, I realize that God was always there. Rather then looking at what happened, my reality was focused on what did not happen and the good things that were actually happening in my life.

As someone having gone through an abusive situation and would sometimes see themselves as weak, but that perception is not the reality I accept. The perception I recognize is that whatever happened, did not break me and I realize the strength God has given me.

I started out with a WHY ME attitude and a negative outlook, but eventually that changed. I had a cleaning agent to clean my lenses. It did not happen overnight, but my vision became clear...no longer distorted with a negative perception and reality. I stopped seeing the victim and saw the VICTOR. I did not see a weakling, but I saw a warrior.

My vision change...my perception changed...and my language changed

So, today, I encourage you to:

- Have a desire to see clearly. Looking at life through dirty lenses and unclear vision is unhealthy for the mind, body, and soul
- Be bold like Bartimaeus. You have three stories before you of how Jesus helped to restore vision. Dare to cry out to Jesus for help too. He can heal you just like He has done for us and so many others.
- Stay before God as He continues to work on you.

Fresh Manna: Journey To A New Beginning

- As your vision is changed...you must change your language.
- Submit a prayer request (to me), and I will pray with you.

Readings: Mark 8:22-26, Mark 10:46-52

Reflections:

1. Do you see the world through the lens of your past?
2. Do you focus on negativity, pain, and suffering?
3. When approached with a new situation or opportunity, do you first think of a previously related situation/opportunity that did not go well/end well?
4. Do you take what you have learned from previous situations and continue to move forward?
5. Is your focus why me? Is your language reflection of why me?
6. What is your testimony?
7. Are you telling your testimony?

DAY THIRTEEN: BE YE DIFFERENT

Being original is important. You cannot afford to be just like every and anyone else. Some of these folks you want to copy are disobedient, not following God's plans, directions, orders and your obedience and originality may very well make them obsolete.

You may think that your "original" thoughts or ideas will make you obscure, but this is not true.

You were hidden, unseen for a reason and season. This was your preparation season. During this time, your eyes were opened, your heart was opened, and your mind was opened to what God was training/preparing you for.

Now the time is soon to come where you will need to step forward. It may very well feel like God is pushing you, but you will need to bring all the original things He gave you.

As God gave me this, this morning, He brought to mind the youth...well let's say the younger generation.

These are some of the greatest minds, but they are talked about, underestimated, misunderstood, and overlooked. The truth is, they are just different. They see the world differently than most in the older generations do. These young people have been dealing with "devils" that most of us could never imagine, but they have not necessarily received the assistance from the elders they must respect and honor.

It's ok though because God sees all. He sees how the elders are either not there for them or too busy trying to change them. Trying to make little clones out of them. Meanwhile, God has been raising up a new generation of leaders. They are a new generation of forerunners.

These are the same people who were overlooked or "oppressed" for being original...for seeing and thinking differently. Meanwhile, those who wanted to treat them as drones and clones will fade into the background for they were nothing but clones themselves. Never having the courage to be original themselves. Mistaking their disobedience and unoriginality for tradition. They will either ride the wave or get swept away by it.

As this season continues to come upon us, I encourage you to remember that there is NOTHING wrong with you for being original...daring to be different. It will get you way further than being a carbon copy...a doppelganger...a look alike/sound alike...a replica of every and anyone else.

God does not speak His thoughts and ideas to you to waste His breath. It is all a part of His plan and purpose for you.

Be original and be obedient to how and what He is asking of you.

Reflections:

1. How do you stand out? Do you think differently? See things differently? Have different ideas on how things should be?
2. Do you hide in the background or pushed to the side because you are different?
3. Why is it so hard to be different? What are the rewards of being different?
4. Why has God called you to be different?

DAY FOURTEEN: WHAT IS YOUR SOURCE?

What god can help you?
Faced with challenges……
Looking around at the world around you…constant drama on the news…killings, shootings, kidnappings, fires, sickness, robberies, fightings.

How can you possibly find true direction and guidance? Nothing seems to make any sense anymore.

There has to be answers somewhere…at least an answer for me
I just need to know what I am doing…
What can I do…where am I going…where is my life headed

These are questions that plague many people but where are we all turning for answers?

The lost are looking, unfortunately to the lost, for a glimpse of hope. But, if I am lost too, can I really help you? Not likely.

I listen to many people relating to who they are and where they seek answers:
Astrology ({greek}zodiac {gods}, horoscopes)
Psychics
spiritual guides
The universe
Fortune tellers

When and why did we ever begin to subject ourselves to these sources? Not realizing who we were and

Fresh Manna: Journey To A New Beginning
conforming to the identification of a "sign?"

What if I told you that there is a story in the Bible that helps you see that these sources cannot help you? These sources cannot truly unlock things for you to help you.

Daniel 1-2:1-30

Around 605 BC, King Nebuchadnezzar of Babylon besieged Jerusalem and took into captivity many of Jerusalem's wisest men and women. The captives were taken to the temple of his god.
The children of Israel were thought to be of value and promise, so they were taught and trained in the ways and language of the Chaldeans (those who ruled Babylon).
The primary academia in this area/culture was focused on math, history, science, astronomy, and magic.

This brings me to Daniel (and his friends). They were among these children. Given names with strong meanings,at birth, their names were changed by the king. He wanted them to have a Babylonian identity.

Why is this important?
When you were born, you were given an identity too. Although Daniel and his friends did not want to become captives to the Babylonians, neither do we want to be captives to anything. Unfortunately, we allow ourselves to do so anyway as we give in to other gods. We serve gods like the zodiac gods and take on a new identity. We were never meant to serve these gods created under Greek mythology.

Under the God that Daniel served, his name meant, "God is my judge," but his new name, Belteshazzar, meant "Bel, protect his life." Bel was the chief Babylonian god.

Here are the conversions of his friends:
Hananiah – the Lord shows grace, his new name Shadrach meant, under the command of Aku (the moon god)
Mishael- who is like God? His new name, Meshach meant, who is like Aku
Azariah – the Lord helps. His new name Abed-nego means the servant of Nego/Nebo (the god of learning and writing)

How does this compare to now?

Individuality is wrapped in

- "I am a Gemini," thought to be misunderstood because of their dual personality expressed by the "twins" of their sign. Why would anyone want to be identified as having a dual personality? Plus, you are already condemning yourself to a life of negativity because by this identity you are the "most understood."

- "I am a Sagittarius," represented by a half human and half horse creature. I think that is enough said there.

- "I am a Virgo," ruled by Mercury, a bundle of energy, considered worrywarts that do their best to temper impulses. If nervousness goes unchecked could lead to hypochondria. Sounds like destiny for anxiety, to me.

Let's get back to the story and fast-forward.

In the second year of his reign, the king has a disturbing dream that no one can interpret for him. Mind you that in his court, he is surrounded by magicians, astrologers, sorcerers, and Chaldeans. Back then the astrologers could give some sort of interpretation of the dream as long as they knew WHAT THE DREAM WAS ABOUT?
Now, wait a minute...sounds like the same sources (psychics, spiritual guides, etc.) some people still put their faith and trust in, doesn't it?
If I need an interpretation (understanding, explanation, or meaning of something) and you can supposedly unlock truth, why do I need to give you most of the revelation to start? Something is not right here.

Apparently, the king felt the same way because he refused to give in. Seems he was testing the authentic "powers" of his court of "wise men." None of them could provide him answers, and the king is ready to slay all the wise men of Babylon.

After finding out what was happening, Daniel went to the One that could honestly give revelation and unlock things that no one else could. He went to God, for he understood that wisdom and might are His. He knew that God gives knowledge and reveals the deep and secret things.

Upon seeking the Lord, this same wisdom was granted to Daniel and he thanked Him for revealing the king's matter. He was able to do what none of these so-called "wise men" could do. He provided the interpretation to the king, from God. Before telling both the dream and interpretation, Daniel first explained this to the king:

"Daniel answered before the king and said, "As for the mystery about which the king has
inquired, neither wise men, conjurers, magicians nor diviners are able to declare it to the king. " However, there is a God in heaven who reveals mysteries, and He has made known to King Nebuchadnezzar what will take place in the latter days." (Daniel 2:27-28)

What is my point?

I understand that in desperate times, we want answers? We want an explanation for
Why we feel a certain way
What we are feeling
What we should do in situations
What is the best course of action
Sometimes, without realizing it, we just want or need to identify with something to give peace of mind.

I get it, I really do (I have been there) but the best source is God for:

Answers – Isaiah 64:4, says, I will answer them before they even call to me. While they are still talking about their needs, I will go ahead and answer their prayers! (NLT)
TRUE PEACE of mind – I Peter 5:7, Cast all your anxiety on him because he cares for you
Guidance – Psalm 31:3, For You are my rock and my

fortress; For Your name's sake You will lead me and guide me
Your identity – John 1:12, Yet to all who did receive

him, to those who believed in his name, he gave the right to become children of God- (NIV)

Do not seek false gods...UNITE WITH THE ONE TRUE GOD. He is the ONLY GOD that can help you!

Psalm 20 (MSG)
For the music leader. A psalm of David.

20 I pray that the Lord answers you
whenever you are in trouble.
Let the name of Jacob's God protect you.
2 Let God send help to you from the sanctuary
and support you from Zion.
3 Let God recall your many grain offerings;
let him savor your entirely burned offerings. Selah
4 Let God grant what is in your heart
and fulfill all your plans.
5 Then we will rejoice that you've been helped.
We will fly our flags in the name of our God.
Let the Lord fulfill all your requests!
6 Now I know that the Lord saves his anointed one;
God answers his anointed one
from his heavenly sanctuary,
answering with mighty acts of salvation
achieved by his strong hand.
7 Some people trust in chariots, others in horses;
but we praise the Lord's name.
8 They will collapse and fall,
but we will stand up straight and strong.
9 Lord, save the king!
Let him answer us when we cry out!

Readings: Daniel 1-2:1-30, Psalm 20, Isaiah 64:4, I Peter 5:7, Psalm 31:3, John 1:12

Reflections:

1. What guides your day?
2. Do you still find help in reading horoscopes? If so, study (objectively) your "sign."
3. Where did it come from? What was it created to mean?
4. Does this really identify you or have you given into that identity?
5. How do you obtain answers to the things you seek?
6. Do you believe that God still speaks? Why or why not?
7. How does God speak to you?
8. How can you spend more time with God to hear the answers you need?

Fresh Manna: Journey To A New Beginning

DAY FIFTEEN: DOUBLE LIFE

I dance, I shout, I read my Bible...
I am a heavy drinker, a smoker, I use foul language
I go to church EVERY Sunday...
I frequent bars and strip clubs
I tell people how much I love God...
I give thanks to God in public for all the "things" He has given me: the money, the cars, and notoriety
When you make me angry, I will curse you out in a heartbeat...
I am not one to play with...I am quick-tempered...a proclaimed hot head
On Sunday mornings I put on my fancy clothes and smile...
I greet everyone with that famous church hug and tell you how Blessed and highly favored I am
I know all the church songs...
I've got all the move down
I am married, I preached The Gospel...
I show off all my family portraits
People know me a Pastor, Preacher, Teacher, a man/woman of God

I am authoritative, but I use that to bully. I rule with a heavy hand for I am far from realizing that my unresolved past has caused me to oppress those I am supposed to shepherd or lead out of captivity.

To you, I am free...I have it all together, I live in prosperity

But what you do not see is that I am still enslaved to my past, which now manifests as my present. I am still trying to find my way...walking blindly at times, and barely making ends meet.

I lead many people but at home, my family is falling apart, and my own children do not hear my voice when I speak

I AM LIVING A DOUBLE LIFE
This double life, I am living has me constantly tossed between right and wrong, peace and disharmony/calamity, partiality and wholeness. Torn between two worlds, living in the abyss, belonging to neither world...This is not the life...there has to be more...

What are we saying or demonstrating about God when we are living a DOUBLE LIFE?

One thing I have learned through studying and experience is that God is a faithful and just God.

We can try to deceive/fool everyone by attempting to perpetrate the life we want everyone to see BUT GOD does SEE ALL. You are surely not deceiving him.

As the body of Christ, we should be a living example of God's Word. Our life, how we live, what we say...will be the greatest witness to those who have yet to believe.

We must walk faithfully, as we CANNOT be ambassadors of God's kingdom and expecting favor while we demonstrate to the world a life that is far from God.

Let's look at the life of someone who lived a double life: Judas Iscariot

While many will say, I already know the story of Judas...Let's look at it a little differently though.

Let's explore his background a little.

Judas Iscariot- an original disciple of Jesus. He along with the original 11 other apostles, was given authority over unclean spirits, to cast them out, and to cure every disease and every sickness. (Matthew 10:1)

He was given a charge by Jesus to go out to the lost sheep of Israel and proclaim the good news, the Kingdom of heaven has come near. Further instructions were to "cure the sick, raise the dead, cleanse the lepers, cast out demons. YOU RECEIVED WITHOUT PAYMENT; GIVE WITHOUT PAYMENT. Take no gold, or silver, or copper in your belts, no bag for your journey, or two tunics, or sandals, or a staff; for laborers deserve their food." (Matthew 10:6-10)

Concerned more about his needs rather than his commission, which was a privilege to receive from Christ, Judas sought to do things without Christ and lived a double life.

Walking with Christ and trying to live for those who did not or would not follow The Savior. He decided to be amongst those who would not follow rather than reaching them as he was commissioned.

Then one of the twelve, who was called Judas Iscariot, went to the chief priests and said, What will you give me if I betray him to you? They paid him thirty pieces of silver. And from that moment he began to look for an opportunity to betray Him. (Matthew 26:14-16)

As I stated before, no matter what we try to 'portray" in front of others, God sees all. You cannot hide your true self /your heart from Him.

The evening during the Passover meal, Jesus said, "Truly I tell you, one of you will betray me." And they [the twelve] became greatly distressed and began to say to him one after another, "Surely not I, Lord?" He answered, "The one who has dipped his hand into the bowl with me will portray me. The Son of Man goes as it is written of him, but woe to the one whom the Son of Man is betrayed! It would have been better for that one not to have been born." Judas, who betrayed him, said, "Surely not I, Rabbi?" He replied, "You have said so." (Matthew 26:21-25)

After Jesus' arrest and those who conspired against him conferred about bringing about his death, Judas, seeing what was accomplished by his double life began to feel guilty, possible fearful, and confused. The Bible tells us that he repented and tried to give back the thirty pieces of silver. He said to the priests and elders, "I have sinned by betraying innocent blood."

Isn't something how those who gave him the silver, did not want it back. They knew that this silver, tainted, could not be returned to the treasury.

(NOTE: the treasury (of the Temple) was where sacred things were kept. This is where items offered to God were stowed. Items like tithes and spoils of war dedicated to Yahweh)

So naturally, this silver could not be returned to such a "sacred" place. The only use the priests could agree on was to create a potter's field.

The potter's field was where the indigent were buried. People who are considered strangers, criminals, these people do not belong anywhere.

Back to Judas:

Not accepted by the priests, they cared not that he lived this double life and that his life caused him to go against God. Instead, he would be forever associated with a place where the vagrant would be buried. Those who did not belong to anyone or anywhere...They were without a "home."

See, this is what happens when you are living a double life. You have no allegiance as you cannot align yourself with both right and wrong. You, as much you try to portray to others, have walked with Christ but you do not belong to Him any further. You have not committed to being with and in Him. You have yet to allow Him to set a place in his kingdom for you. Why? Because you are also walking with those who oppose Him but they do not want you either because you have not fully committed to them either. You belong nowhere...You are an indigent person....living faithfully to no one.

Stay with me ... It is important to see the flip side and examine one who lived faithfully to God

Caleb, you can read his story in Numbers 13, 14, and Deuteronomy.

He along with others were also given a commission. They were sent to spy out the land of Canaan. This was the land promised to the Israelites. After spending forty days in Canaan, the men returned and brought back fruits of the land as directed. Yet, they also brought back a "bad" report fearing the people who were already established there. But Caleb, stood faithful. Yes, since he went out as a spy, one can say, well he too lived a double life BUT do not miss what's a significant difference. Caleb walked with God, he lived faithfully doing the work of The Lord. He understood his commission, and when others feared those they were to conquer, he knew that if God sent him, he and the people would prevail. Even as others faltered, he stood firmly on God's Word. For this, Caleb found favor with God.

See, a faithful man who walks with God will be able to see what God is showing them but an unfaithful man, trying to live a double life is blinded as he is too busy trying to see for himself.

How can you focus if you are so busy running back and forth between two lives you are attempting to live? You cannot ...you are too preoccupied.

Caleb didn't have to try to control the situation or the people he was sent with. Rather he just believed God for he knew Him. He relayed what God promised and challenged their faith, but he did not forcefully do so. In fact, the people threatened to stone him for saying such things.

This is the message God gave Moses concerning Caleb: "But my servant Caleb, because he has a different spirit and has followed me wholeheartedly, I will bring into the land into which he went, and his descendants shall possess it." (Numbers 14:24)

There is no reward for living a double life. There is only suffering and a rejected offering. Don't be a Judas, be a Caleb. Follow God faithfully for this is what He wants, expects, and will honor. Find your way to Christ and stop worrying about looking good in the eyes of man. They cannot save you, only Christ can. In Him, you can have a real home and a NEW LIFE.

Readings: Matthew 10:1-10, Matthew 26:14-25, Numbers 13, 14

Reflections:

1. Are you being true to yourself 100% of the time or are you wearing a mask depending on who you are with?
2. Are you the same at work, at school, around family and friends, at church or have you just learned how to play the game well? Would God agree with you, based on what He sees?

ENJOY THE JOURNEY

The most Incredible Journeys start out fantastic, but along the road, you may get tired or a little weary. You begin to wonder,
   Am I going to make it
   Can make it the rest of the way
   Is this even worth it any more
BUT once you take a moment to stop, TAKE A breathe and remember what lies ahead, or why you made the decision to start the journey, you can begin to focus on the beauty of it all rather than the number of steps it will take you to finish.

Take it ALL in, experience the beauty of your journeys. What did you learn along the way? Who are you meeting along the way? What new things have you learned about yourself along the way?

Were you stronger than you thought? Were you smarter than you thought?
Have you found kind and loving people or have you focused only on those who were not there for you?

Has your perspective on life changed any? Have you become more mature? Have you learned to appreciate life's most precious moments more or are you letting them pass you by because you're still focusing on all the negative and stressful things?

Keep pressing along your journey for even when the climb seems a little harsh, there is still beauty in it all.

Take it in and do not miss out on the important things along the way.

DAY SIXTEEN: NO UNDERDOGS HERE

The Underdog - the one counted out, the one least likely to win or achieve, or the one incapable or unworthy of being able to handle the greatest tasks. Many see the underdog as the weaker one, therefore, expecting very little from them. In fact, the definition of the underdog is:
A competitor thought to have little chance of winning in a fight or contest. A person who has low status in society.

Wow, low in stature according to the eyes and thoughts of those around. What a way to be perceived.

BUT the underdog should never be counted out. In fact, because there is a GOD who can do all things, I would say, that these underdogs are actually THE Overcomers, much like Gideon.

This young man found working in an area hidden from view...an unsuspected place was called by God to do the unexpected.

Not considered strong or in a prestigious position in the sight of man, yet call a Mighty Man of Valor by God.

God called upon Gideon, during an unexpected time.

The People of Israel were not honoring God, and due to how God allowed them to live. As a result, the people were desperate. Being the merciful and gracious God He is, He still heard and answered the prayers of his chosen people.

God chose Gideon to carry out His plan but just because God chose Gideon did not mean that any or everyone acknowledged this. In fact, as you read Judges 8:1-12, you can see the times in which Gideon was mocked and even scolded for what he knew God told him to do. When Gideon asked for help, he was turned away and taunted.

This is much like some of you. God has shared things with you about His plan for your life, things you would do and achieve, places you would go and see, but it seems that people just consider you a DREAMER.

You have had some rough times, some setbacks and all while you have been working so hard, meanwhile watched so many others rise to the top. You have been working in the background watching many stake their claim to fame. You have wondered, when will it be my time.

You have asked for help along the road but those who have "made it" just continue to overlook you. You have been considered not worthy...you're at the bottom of the totem pole...you're not strong enough, not wise enough. You have been treated as the underdog and left in the back of the room or on the outside of the circle but let me tell you what God sees.

God sees that you have been listening to Him and have not given up. Yes, you may have been frightened at times to step out when He says so BUT you do.
Yes, people mock and taunt you, BUT you have hung in there.
Yes, people have stepped over you or turned away from

Fresh Manna: Journey To A New Beginning

you BUT you continue to hang in there
Yes, people have counted you out because they do not see you in "the spotlight."
Yes, you may have some failures
Yes, they called you the underdog
 But GOD sees THE OVERCOMER!

God sees the one who pressed through their circumstances and believing what HE said
God sees the one who was obedient to follow HIS instructions
God sees the one who was humble enough to keep working even when no one else noticed or acknowledged what was being done
God sees the one who, like Gideon was working down in the pit, the unseen area, and sending prayers to God.

When Gideon's time came, despite his own judgment or fear, his humility, obedience, and faith in God are what God honored.

STAY IN THE FIGHT...YOU'RE NOT AN UNDERDOG...YOU ARE AN OVERCOMER

Woe to those who have counted you out because your time is far from being over...YOU ARE JUST TRULY GETTING STARTED

Readings: Judges 8:1-12

Reflections:

1. As you read Judges 8:1-12 about Gideon, how can you relate to Gideon's story?

2. How do you see God using you? Can you see Him using you in a way others would not imagine or think? Maybe they are unaware of how capable you are.
3. What gifts have God blessed you with that others are unaware of?
4. How is God using your gifts, in the background?

DAY SEVENTEEN: WHAT'S IT WORTH TO YOU?

What if God gave you a dream and told you that this was not just a dream but a glimpse of your future? What would it be worth to you to have it come true? What if you knew you were on the verge of success, but you would have to give up something to reach that final place?

What if...

true happiness was presented to you, but to have it, you had to sell your worldly possessions and move to a new place...would you do it?

the big break in your career was on the horizon, but you had to give up even more time when it seems you already do not have enough time in a day...would you be willing to give up an hour or two of sleep a night?

if you were told, that the great finish line, whatever it was you were asking for or desperately seeking, was just over the horizon, would you dig deep enough, forgetting how tired you were and be willing to climb it no matter the cost?

if to receive a blessing, you had to go back and face the one you offended, hurt, or misused...would you be able to put your pride aside and go?

What is the end...your goal...your breakthrough all worth to you?

I am reminded of Jacob and the dream that God gave him in Genesis 28:13-15 (NRSV)

"And the Lord stood beside him and said, "I am the Lord, the God of Abraham your father and the God of Isaac; the land on which you lie I will give to you and your offspring shall be like the dust of the earth, and you shall spread abroad to the west and to the east and to the north and to the south; and all the families of the earth shall be blessed in you and in your offspring. Know that I am with you and will keep you wherever you go, and will bring you back to this land; for I will not leave you until I have done what I promised you."

Now, when the time came, and God told Jacob to return to the land of his father, he was afraid for he thought his brother would kill him. Why? Because years before, Jacob fled after deceiving his father to steal his brother's birthright and blessing, therefore, his brother desired to slay him. (Genesis 27:1-40) (That is the short, simple version)

Could you imagine, now being told that you will now need to return back to this place and face your brother?

Jacob deathly afraid, still did what God instructed and prepared to return to Canaan and along the way, he had an encounter with God. The story tells of how he wrestled with God all night, but the significance here is that Jacob was persistent. He was going to give EVERYTHING he had and do WHATEVER it took to get his blessing from God.

Genesis 32:26-29 (ESV)

26 Then he said, "Let me go, for the day has broken."

But Jacob said, "I will not let you go unless you bless me." 27 And he said to him, "What is your name?" And he said, "Jacob." 28 Then he said, "Your name shall no longer be called Jacob, but Israel, for you have striven with God and with men, and have prevailed." 29 Then Jacob asked him, "Please tell me your name." But he said, "Why is it that you ask my name?" And there he blessed him.

When Jacob reached home, the UNEXPECTED happened, his brother Esau, ran to meet him with open arms and an open heart. All was well, and peace was made.

Later Jacob would return to Bethel, the place where God initially gave him the dream. He decided to make some additional changes to his life. After having many trials and difficulties throughout his life, Jacob realized that God was the one that met him in his time of despair. He decided to stay close to God, and the even greater happened...the fulfillment of the promise.

Genesis 35:11-12 (NIV)

11 And God said to him, "I am God Almighty; be fruitful and increase in number. A nation and a community of nations will come from you, and kings will be among your descendants. 12 The land I gave to Abraham and Isaac I also give to you, and I will give this land to your descendants after you.

Jacob went through much just to receive the blessings and promises of God. He even went to face his brother who he thought would kill him, wrestled all night with

God, and gave up his old life and habits. To him, it was all worth it.

WHAT IS IT ALL WORTH TO YOU?

What sacrifices are you willing to make? Are you willing to do the UNEXPECTED to receive the UNEXPECTED?

Readings: Genesis 27:1-40, 28:13-15, 32:26-29, 35:11-12

Reflections:

1. What is your goal or your breakthrough worth to you?
2. What are you willing to sacrifice to receive what God has for you?
3. Could you sacrifice what looks like the promise to receive more or are you holding on to it so tightly there is no room to receive anything else?

DAY EIGHTEEN: HE WILL WORK IT OUT

This morning, I kept hearing this song, God will work it out. Now, at first, I was thinking, that's not how the song goes. When I searched through my music, there was another version than what I remember listening to growing up. This one is by Tye Tribbett. Now, I am listening...over and over and over again. I get it!! I understand what God was saying...

Romans 8:18-30 (MSG)
18-21 That's why I don't think there's any comparison between the present hard times and the coming good times. The created world itself can hardly wait for what's coming next. Everything in creation is being more or less held back. God reins it in until both creation and all the creatures are ready and can be released at the same moment into the glorious times ahead. Meanwhile, the joyful anticipation deepens.

22-25 All around us we observe a pregnant creation. The difficult times of pain throughout the world are simply birth pangs. But it's not only around us; it's within us. The Spirit of God is arousing us within. We're also feeling the birth pangs. These sterile and barren bodies of ours are yearning for full deliverance. That is why waiting does not diminish us, any more than waiting diminishes a pregnant mother. We are enlarged in the waiting. We, of course, don't see what is enlarging us. But the longer we wait, the larger we become, and the more joyful our expectancy.

26-28 Meanwhile, the moment we get tired in the waiting, God's Spirit is right alongside helping us along. If we don't know how or what to pray, it doesn't matter. He does our praying in and for us, making prayer out of our wordless sighs, our aching groans. He knows us far better than we know ourselves, knows our pregnant condition, and keeps us present before God. That's why we can be so sure that every detail in our lives of love for God is worked into something good.

29-30 God knew what he was doing from the very beginning. He decided from the outset to shape the lives of those who love him along the same lines as the life of his Son. The Son stands first in the line of humanity he restored. We see the original and intended shape of our lives there in him. After God made that decision of what his children should be like, he followed it up by calling people by name. After he called them by name, he set them on a solid basis with himself. And then, after getting them established, he stayed with them to the end, gloriously completing what he had begun.

I have read this passage so many times, but it is something about this particular version in the message Bible.

This past year, I have met so many people who shared stories about the challenges they have been facing whether it was health, finances, family situations, etc. They have been praying and seeking prayers of others to get through these times. Many of them struggled with their faith as it just seemed that it would only get worse and not better OR just when it seemed to get better, something else came along...the suffering was just not letting up.

BUT I just want to encourage you today to NOT STOP PRAYING. The Word of God says that the sufferings of this present time are not worthy to be compared with the glory which shall be revealed in us.

Like the mother who goes through pregnancy, those nine months are not the glorious times. In fact, it can be quite rough. The glory comes when the child is born...the GIFT at the end and knowing that God was there ALL along, WORKING IT OUT.

Listen, we really need to STOP putting limits on God's POWER. It is time to start believing God for the GREATER ...THE UNEXPECTED...THE UNIMAGINABLE. That is what He wants...That is what He is about to show us.

Great things are coming for the people of God...

Believe He will WORK IT OUT...whatever the situation is:

Have not had a job...He will work it out

Have not been in the best of health...He will work it out

The family has been falling apart...He will work it out

That MIRACLE you have been praying for...He will work it out

BELIEVE IN THE POWER OF GOD...There is NOTHING too hard for Him

For when the work is done, you shall never doubt again

Readings: *Romans 8:18-30*

Reflections:

This is where you get to reflect on the difficult situations that seem unbearable, never-ending, or just kicking your butt, at times. These are the things you believe God will work out for you. Write them down, give them to God and move forward. Later, you can return to this point and write how God has worked each one out for you.

DAY NINETEEN: THE GREATEST LOVE

This has been, to say the least, an interesting week. I want to share with you something that happened this week and how God will take an any and everyday situation to teach a lesson.

For the past few weeks, I have been contemplating a way to get my hair braided. After finally making a decision and weeks of finding someone who was able to provide what I wanted, I finally set an appointment.

On Monday evening, I was given a time for Tuesday at 10am. This meant that I now had to sit up, take the previous braids down and prepare for the next day. Typically, it does not take me long, but this night, I was up until 3am.

Tuesday morning, I go to my 10 am appointment, get my hair done, it looks great, and I proceed with the rest of my day. Twelve hours later, I start having a reaction to extensions used to create the style I wanted. I ended up contacting my stylist, who was very kind and understanding, to explain what's happening. I get some advice from her and proceed with taking most of my hair down. Again I am up until 3am. I am tired, frustrated, annoyed and honestly in pain. I get some relief from removing what was causing pain but able to keep what was not.

The next morning, I proceed BACK to my stylist who had room for me to come back and at the same time...10am. She was understanding and began to work again. This time, she did not have to do as much work as the day prior because half the work was still already done. Through the process, she kept checking on me to make sure I was ok and not having another reaction to what was now being used. I appreciated the comfort.

Hours later, I leave even more satisfied than the day prior. Again proceeded through the remainder of my day and went to church that evening. We had a fantastic service, BUT hours later when I returned home, it started again SUDDENLY and at 10pm no less.

What in the world is happening?! I am devastated because of the pain due to the reaction. I just go and start trying to take my hair down AGAIN.

Up until 3am once again, I decided enough is enough. I give up...forget it...I have no idea what happened or why all I know is that I am entirely OVER IT.

I let my stylist know what happened and wanted to thank her for all of her work. I said thank you because although it looked great, it was just not working out yet it was not her fault. I wanted her to know that I would still give her the best review on her site, for her work and that prayerfully the remaining under braids would hold up for now.

Unexpectedly, I get a phone call from her, and the message said that what was "left behind" that I planned on using, would not hold. She said that if I could come in around 3pm, she would see what she could do to help me. She gave me directions to prepare myself for my appointment and I followed them and arrived at my time.

She redid my hair BUT not in the way I contemplated about over the first several weeks. What she gave me was not what I planned on, it was not what I thought I wanted, it was nothing I would have come up with on my own, in fact, it was WAY BETTER.

Once she was done, I asked her, "how much?"

She said, not to worry about it...I had been through enough. (To keep this honest, know that I paid for the supplies BUT it is important to stay focused on the fact that I did not have to pay the price for her services)

I was overwhelmed and thankful. I offered a prayer before I left, as God was pressing that upon my heart while I was sitting in the chair. I now understood why...

Now, here is what I want to point out...My stylist, goes by the name Love.

Later that evening, while speaking with someone, talking about my day, I felt like God was saying...DID YOU GET IT YET? And did I ever...

Although I spent so much time trying to figure out what I wanted, when I wanted it, and where I would get it from, none of that worked out for me.

What did work out was that with everything I went through and was going through, ON THE THIRD

DAY, LOVE GAVE ME SOMETHING
I DID NOT PLAN FOR,
I DID NOT THINK I NEEDED
I DID NOT THINK I WANTED, and
I CERTAINLY DID NOTHING TO EARN

In fact, what I did receive was better than what I planned and wanted. Best of all, the service was PAID IN FULL

This is how it is in life...

We plan out things, they do not go the way we want, then we go to God asking for help. When we go back, we do not want to let go of everything, to allow God to truly work in us or on us. We try to hold on to those things we think will STILL WORK. Then when it doesn't, we get tired and frustrated. We want to give up...

When people then ask you about God, we usually say, well...I am sure He exists, but I guess "the whole God thing is just not for me."

What is wonderful about God is that His Love knows no boundaries and is never-ending

We do so much in our lives, and we give up on God BUT He has NEVER given up on us. He is always there trying to show us how much He LOVES us. He keeps trying to show us that through His LOVE, there is so much more waiting for us. He wants us to be reconciled and aligned with Him. What did we do to deserve this? Absolutely NOTHING.

We see this scripture everywhere:

John 3:16, "For God so loved the world that he gave his one and only Son, that whoever believes in him shall not perish but have eternal life."

But have you ever really stopped to reflect on that? Have you stopped to think of the magnitude of His Love?

How about reflecting on the death and resurrection of Christ?

What a LOVE that would go through the suffering He did for us. Even those who walked with Him while He was in the flesh, ran away when Christ was arrested, and crucified. Yet, He still showed LOVE.

On the THIRD day, He ROSE...Resurrected from the grave signifying a new life we can have with Him.

God has never stopped loving us, His love is unconditional, and through HIS LOVE, there is much offered:

There is no fear in love, but perfect love casts out fear. Love SAVES, Love Delivers (sets you free), Love Heals, LOVE NEVER FAILS and the price of LOVE has already been paid.

I don't know about you but this Love, God's Love is a love that I do not want to live without for God is indeed the Greatest Love of ALL.

Reflections:

1. What does it mean to have God's love?
2. What would you do without God's love? What would your life be like without God's love?
3. Knowing how much God loves you, how can you show your love for Him?

DAY TWENTY: PROMISES... PROMISES... PROMISES

What happens when the journey does not look like the given Promise? You activate your FAITH!

Years ago, God made a promise to the children of Israel that He would free them from captivity, delivering them from the hands of their enemy and lead them to the promise land - Canaan.

Time after time, due to what they saw in front of them, they could not imagine the promise being fulfilled. They continued to doubt that God would do exactly what He said He would do.

Even when God delivered them from the strongholds of the pharaoh, they still complained, doubted, and spoke bitterly against God.

Despite this, God still provided for them. The path was set before them, and all provisions were made. While making their trek through the wilderness, they quickly forgot how God saved them. Initially, they danced and praised God after they made it through the Red Sea. When they went into the wilderness of Shur, after three days, they started the complaining again, for they were thirsty.

This is what we do as God's children. We cry and lose all hope and faith regarding the promise while we are busy focused on the little things that pop up along the way. We forget to dance and praise God along the way except for the times when we actually see Him do the little things. Then we go back to whining and complaining when we, again, hit the next step along the journey.

When the children were thirsty, God provided...when they were hungry, God provided. Each time, the children were still quick to complain before they allowed God do what He said He would do.

These children disobeyed God, began to worship other gods...If we saw children who are disobedient, quick to anger, always complaining, and whining all the time, we would be quick to call them UNGRATEFUL.

You ever see a kid in a store (or this applies to you and your child if you have them) and a parent says, "I will get it for you later...You can have it after..., etc." Then you see the child throw a tantrum because it is not happening now and they are just tired of waiting? In fact, the wait really has not been long before the tears come.

It's not that the parent will not keep their word or even has not kept their word in the past. It's that the child is too impatient to wait, does not believe in the word of the parent, or a combination of both. (Well they could also just be a spoiled brat)

Wait, is this how we are with God? Nothing is ever enough...we just complain, quit, whine, and turn our back on God.

What I love about God is that despite how we treat Him, HE never gives up on us. When He gives a promise, He is not like us, wavering or forgetting. NO! He keeps His promises.

Fresh Manna: Journey To A New Beginning

When we hurt Him, turning away, serving other gods, He keeps His promise. In fact, He LOVES us so much that He keeps sending the seen and unseen messages to guide us back on the pathway He set down for us.

God is patient, but when you read this story, it is apparent that His patience was, to say the least, TRIED. Much like we say our children (in our lives) do to us - trying the patience.

God is FAITHFUL even though we are NOT...He keeps His WORD...His Promise

He delivered the children of Israel out of Egypt to Canaan, the land promised. It is fair to say that they really did not even deserve it considering their actions, their lack of faith and lack of faithfulness to Him but, He stayed FAITHFUL. He promised, laid out the pathway, and made provisions all along the way.

For the promise God gave you, I am sure the journey makes it seem like the promise will not come to pass. Rest and know that if God gave it to you, He will get you to it.

Do not doubt, do not complain, do not lose hope, do not begin to rely on or make other gods...Just say, "Yet, I will TRUST YOU, GOD!" Let Him hear that you know that:
He is a God that does not lie
He is a God that keeps His Promise
He is a Faithful God, even when we are not

Do not focus on the looks of the journey BUT PRAISE

HIM NOW FOR THE PROMISE

Reflections:

1. Reflect on the journey to your promise. How has it been? What does the way ahead look like?
2. God has made a promise that He will keep. What promises have you made to God? Have you kept them?
3. Has God been faithful to you even in times of your unfaithfulness to Him? How?

STAGE V: COME...SEEK...FIND

There is HOPE for those who seek HOPE

There is HEALING for those who seek HEALING

There is GRACE for those who seek GRACE

There is LOVE for those who seek LOVE

There is MERCY for those who seek MERCY

For there is much in the well for those who thirst

The well cannot run dry for it has no end

It has no bottom...it continues to go on infinitely

Like a Black Hole in deep space that goes on forever

But this well brings life rather than allowing all to be lost

What do you NEED?

What do you ask for?

Come...Come to the well but do not come wishing

Fresh Manna: Journey To A New Beginning

Come in FAITH...believing

Believing in your Heart that, that which you seek, Ye Shall Find

FIND IN CHRIST JESUS!

DAY TWENTY-ONE: WOLF OR SHEEP

It never fails, as soon as it seems that you have been trucking along and about to make a breakthrough, here comes the devil.

He knows just when God is bringing you through and about to open new doors for you. He starts trying to open up old ones. Sending temptation and distraction.

This can only work if you are not mindful AND if you fail to stay at the top of your game. It is important to notice what season you are in and what God is doing or about to do in your life so that you do not get thrown off course.

After Jesus was baptized, He was led by the Spirit into the wilderness. There he fasted for forty days and nights in preparation for the test coming his way. At the end, when He was at the point of hunger, the first test of temptation was presented.

> [3] *The tempter came and said to him, "If you are the Son of God, command these stones to become loaves of bread."* [4] *But he answered, "It is written, 'One does not live by bread alone, but by every word that comes from the mouth of God.'" (Matthew 4:3-4, NRSV)*

Rather than giving in to this temptation, Jesus knew that the nourishment from what the stones (turned to bread) could provide was nothing as great as the nourishment he receives from God. That nourishment comes from God's great and powerful Word. God's Word will always sustain you.

Then came the 2nd test of temptation:

> *⁵ Then the devil took him to the holy city and placed him on the pinnacle of the temple, ⁶ saying to him, "If you are the Son of God, throw yourself down; for it is written, 'He will command his angels concerning you,' and 'On their hands they will bear you up, so that you will not dash your foot against a stone." ⁷ Jesus said to him, "Again it is written, 'Do not put the Lord your God to the test." (Matthew 4:5-7, NRSV)*

Just like where some of you are now, people are coming in or around you, mocking you for what you believe God has told you. They ridicule you and try to get you to test God. You may hear things like: "well if God really said this then blah blah blah…If you really believe then blah blah…Are you sure that is what you are supposed to be doing…" I'm sure we have all heard this or something similar.

Do not fall into this snare.
Stay focused and do not let yourself be drawn in and begin to "test" God and his Word. You need not prove yourself or your God to them. This is not them desiring to get to know The God you serve. This is just an attempt to engage you in their mockery. God is not to be mocked.

The final test of temptation:

> *⁸ Again, the devil took him to a very high mountain and showed him all the kingdoms of the world and their splendor; ⁹ and he said to him, "All these I will give you, if you will fall down and worship me." ¹⁰ Jesus said to him, "Away with you, Satan! for it is written,*

*'Worship the Lord your God, and serve only him.'"
(Matthew 4:8-10, NRSV)*

We have all heard the idiom, "Beware of wolves in sheep clothing." A very common phrase but interestingly enough, this was also a warning in the Bible:

> *15 "Beware of false prophets, who come to you in sheep's clothing but inwardly are ravenous wolves. 16 You will recognize them by their fruits. Are grapes gathered from thornbushes, or figs from thistles? 17 So, every healthy tree bears good fruit, but the diseased tree bears bad fruit. 18 A healthy tree cannot bear bad fruit, nor can a diseased tree bear good fruit. 19 Every tree that does not bear good fruit is cut down and thrown into the fire. 20 Thus you will recognize them by their fruits. (Matthew 7:15-20, NRSV)*

This is just like the last temptation. People will come around and try to show you that what they can give you is better than what God has already given or promised you. They want to show you where they can take you, what they can do for you. They can do for you what no one else has ever done for you. BUYER BEWARE! Why would you need to seek further for what God has already placed in front of you? The enemy knows who you are, even if you don't. The enemy knows how great you are, even if you don't. He knows where God is taking you, even if you won't recognize it for yourself. His job is to throw you off of your game, throw you off track, and distract you from the direction God is taking you.

Fresh Manna: Journey To A New Beginning

DO NOT FALL PREY to the wolf.

Jesus knew His Father and understood His Word. He resisted the temptations of the enemy, and with that, the devil left him and angels came and waited on him.

We have to continue to be strong during our journeys. We need to understand when we are being tested (and taunted). We must NOT give in to temptation. We MUST stay on our toes and our "A-game." You do not want to get so close to your promise just to be diverted or thrown off course. Do not eat from the tree that does not bear good fruit or you risk being cut down with them.

Be sensitive to your surroundings. Be mindful of the people who just so happen to POP-UP in your life. Be cognizant of those who left you, hurt you, did not believe in you, talked about you, or even caused you pain, as they try to come and reinsert themselves back in your life.

Remember where God has brought you from, how you have grown, and where you are going. Do you really need these people and situations? No, you needed them back then to allow you to grow in God. Those situations drew you closer to the Father. Now those doors are closed…Think, why would you need to reopen them?

Isaiah 43:18-19 (NRSV)

*18 "Remember not the former things, nor consider the things of old.
19 Behold, I am doing a new thing; now it springs forth,*

Fresh Manna: Journey To A New Beginning

do you not perceive it? I will make a way in the wilderness and rivers in the desert.

Keep moving FORWARD...this is definitely NOT the time to start going BACK

Now is not the time to be foolish...Move cautiously and be wise in your steps, your decisions, and your actions.

Readings: Matthew 4:3-4, 7:15-20, Isaiah 43:18-19

Reflections:

1. To move continuously and be wise in your steps, you must be aware of the strategy of the enemy. Know yourself and your weaknesses. What are they? Who are they?
2. How can the enemy tempt you? What do you want so badly that he can attempt to present to you on a "silver platter?" Begin self-examining now, so you are not caught off guard.

DAY TWENTY-TWO: COME OUT OF THE CLOSET

Are you a closet Christian? Well, it time to COME OUT.

In this day and age with everything going on around us, we cannot afford to deny Christ.

In Matthew 10:33, Jesus states, "But whosoever shall deny Me before men, him will I also deny before my Father which is in heaven." (NKJV)

Let's put your faith to the test: How many times have you witnessed that did not agree with your beliefs, but you decided to ignore it? Now, the bigger question is why? Were you afraid that if you said something, you would "offend" those around you? Were you afraid that if you spoke up, you would be rejected?

Wow, now that is a thought…they could possibly deny you. Why is it so important to fit in with those who have no problem stating what they believe, even if it offends you? What happened to being the leader of the pack, being an individual, or having your own identity?

We have a lot of movements these days that some would consider radical. Everyone is taking a stance for something but who is standing up for Christ?

I could only imagine if we actually spent time focusing on and acknowledging Christ as we did everything else. I mean, look at the things in your life that you are NOT embarrassed about.

The school you attended that you have no qualms sharing that with anyone.
No problems boasting about your favorite sports team as you walk around sporting all of their colors and gear, even if they were the worse team in the league.

We will even defend athletes, celebrities, and politicians for anything and everything they do (right or wrong), even if we are taking the unpopular stance. There is so much pride we take in our worldly alignments, but when it comes to admitting and boasting about Christianity we say:
- Well, I believe in God
- I mean, I am more spiritual than anything else
- I do not believe in religion
- Christianity started wars
- I mean, I believe, but Christians are such hypocrites.

The excuses go on and on, and I truly mean, EXCUSES.

You can deny Christ all you want but your denial does not make Him any less real. Just like, you can deny that a child is your child, but that does not make the child any less real.
There will come a time that we will all have to answer for when we denied Christ but where will that leave you? How will you feel or how will you respond when Jesus denies you because you openly denied him in public?

In fact, where is that leaving us now? In a world of violence, corruption, famine, death, and just repulsive acts committed by man. Where is God...where is Christ? Most would like to blame God for everything, but it's interesting that many will blame the ONE they deny exists. Maybe if so many did not deny Him, curse Him, reject Him, etc., things could actually be a little better.

Maybe if we stop calling on Him like He is some form of genie that we can make a wish on in times of trouble and actually form a relationship with Him, things could be different.

Maybe, just maybe if we stopped being closet Christians, take an open stance, and stop being cowards, our lives could be different. AND perhaps if we actually learned to KEEP God's Commandments, our lives would be more enriched.

Lately, we have seen these posts on social media urging you to share as proof that you are Christian or believe in God. This bully tactic of proving your beliefs does not make you any more of a Christian than putting on a spiderman costume makes you Spiderman. In fact, it is just a mask...something to put on for show. It is what's underneath that actually matters. It is what's in the heart. It's enough to say that you are a good person because some who are murders think they are good people too...just saying. What's underneath must be the core that is rooted in firm beliefs as well as a continually growing relationship with Christ. There must be actions that align with this belief that should follow. There should be the type of relationship you honor so much with your favorite sports teams, where you would show your colors even in the worst of times. How is it that we are more loyal to man than we are to God who actually gave us life?

How or why have we become so ashamed to say the name "Jesus," to pray openly, speak God's Word, and unapologetically worship Him? When are we going to stop allowing any and everyone else to take pride in what they believe yet refuse to stand for our beliefs? When are we going to stop being upset with other religions for their beliefs when we deny Christ at every possible opportunity? Hmmm, guess we really are the hypocrites, and it's just not those in the pulpit that constantly get a bad rap.

We MUST do better. It is time to come out of the closet. Time to stop being, as Jesus said, lukewarm (Revelation 3:16)...confused, wishy-washy, unstable in beliefs. Time to stop denying Christ and BE BOLD FOR JESUS.

Last year, after watching a movie in the theater, when everyone was getting ready to leave, a stranger called out and asked, "Would everyone mind praying together before we leave?" Would you know that everyone literally STOPPED, stood still, bowed heads and was lead in prayer by this man? It was actually a compelling moment. That is how we should all be. Crazy enough to ask the question even if you know you might be rejected for it. Instead, we will not even pray over a meal in public because we do not want to offend others or because "no one else is doing it."

I personally would much rather have the approval of God more than the acceptance of man. Does that make me an outsider at times? Absolutely, but the peace I have is so worth it. Now I just try to spread the news

of who gives me such peace, joy, love and a sound mind so that those around me could have it all too.

I refuse to live in a closet...what about you?

Come out of the closet all ye so-called
Christians...come out from among them and be ye
separate:
Dare to spread the Good News
Dare to spread the Love
Dare to pray with others in need (openly)
Dare to unapologetically follow and worship
Dare to proclaim to others that Jesus is Lord, Savior,
and Redeemer
Do not fear the looks, comments, or rejection of your
fellow-man

Let us NOT be ashamed of The Gospel of Jesus Christ
Seek acceptance from Him and find favor in the eyes of
God

BE BOLD FOR JESUS and watch lives change

Readings: Matthew 10:33, Roman 1:16, Revelations 3:16

Reflections:

1. Are you loudest and proudest about following Christ when around other Christians?
2. What about around those who are not believers or if you are unsure where they stand?
3. Do you acknowledge the goodness of God whenever you have the opportunity or are you doing a temp check of your surroundings first?
4. What is wrong with proclaiming your faith? Why do Christians have such a difficult time proclaiming what they believe?

DAY TWENTY-THREE: FOLLOWER OR DISCIPLE - WHICH ONE ARE YOU?

Have you ever stopped to consider where you are in your walk with Christ? How things could possibly get to a better state? Are you tired of being in a "common" place in your life?

Maybe it is time to reflect and determine if you have just been a FOLLOWER or if you have been a Disciple.

In reading the gospels, certain words stand out, regarding this subject: crowds, multitudes, disciples, and finally apostles.

There was a significance in how the writer of the gospels distinguished between the great multitudes or crowds that followed Jesus and His disciples.

In Luke 6:17, you see one of the distinctions: *"He came down with them and stood on a level place, with a great crowd of his disciples and a great multitude of people from all Judea, Jerusalem, and the coast of Tyre and Sidon."*

As you can see, there are three sets of people present in this text: them (the first called disciples), a great crowd of his disciples, and finally a great multitude of people.

Why was there such a distinction made?

Just like in your personal relationships with people, where some people walk closer with you than others, this was the same for those who walked with Jesus.

As you read, you can see that the CROWDS/multitude that followed Jesus, did so because news had traveled across the lands regarding the signs and wonders He performed, as well as the great teachings He gave. As they (the crowds/multitudes) followed, they came expecting. Many came solely to receive healing and deliverance.

You have seen this, or maybe this has been you. You hear of the new, hot, great thing in the area and you have given everything or done anything just to get a glimpse of it or to be within the circle of those to say, "I was there." You (or they) were just like the crowds following Jesus. Better yet, maybe you have people you know that heard you had something they could use. Suddenly, you become their closest friend as they are now calling you at every instance, wanting to hang out, again, this is only because of what you could do for them. All similar to the crowds/multitudes that followed Jesus.

Interestingly enough, the situation changes when the tables are turned, and they have an opportunity to save you in time of need. They become like the crowds that cried out to let Barabbas, a notorious prisoner who committed murder, go, therefore, not saving Jesus from crucifixion. Let's make it even more personal. We read or hear about the great things Christ can do for us and for that, we FOLLOW Him. When we get what we think we want or need, we leave, until the time returns and we are in need again. We are FOLLOWERS of His work.

At least 24 times in Matthew's Gospel, alone, you will find reference to these crowds. When they followed

Jesus, seeking only healing, deliverance and to hear what he was teaching, they received what they came for. He even fed the great multitudes in the accounted miracles of Jesus feeding the 5000 then the 4000. What happened to the 1000 between here? Why did the crowds get smaller? Did they receive what they wanted and that was enough? They no longer had a need to follow Jesus? Better yet, as you read the accounts in Matthew, you can see that the crowds were the very ones when given an opportunity to help the one who help so many, decided it was best to help the criminal. Seems they were more along the lines of a fan follower. You know how fan followers are? They are only good for the moment we "feel" like following them, then the next thing comes around, and we switch teams.

A disciple is not the same. A disciple is one who does not leave the teacher once they received what they wanted, but taking every opportunity to learn, and has a greater sense of commitment and obedience. Let take a look at the first call of disciples, (Matthew 4:18-22, NRSV).

"As He walked by the Sea of Galilee, He saw two brothers, Simon who is called Peter and Andrew his brother, casting a net into the sea; for they were fishermen. 19 And he said to them, "Follow me, and I will make you fishers of men." 20 Immediately they left their nets and followed him. 21 And going on from there he saw two other brothers, James the son of Zeb'edee and John his brother, in the boat with Zeb'edee their father, mending their nets, and He called them. 22 Immediately they left the boat and their father, and followed Him."

At the drop of a hat, the fisherman dropped all they had and left everything they thought they knew to become one of Christ's disciples. They went wherever Jesus went, they sat and learned from Him. They gained revelation of who He was, not just bombarding Him at every instance. Throughout the scriptures, you can clearly see the distinction. Even in the midst of teaching the crowds, Jesus would be known to pull a particular group aside for additional teaching. Again, you can see the deeper relationship between teacher and disciple.

Yes, they initially followed but they, unlike so many others that followed, they stayed close to Jesus. Yes, we can read about times they were frightened and left Him, but more importantly, you will find how much they really loved Him. Since they were disciples, they adhered to the teachings of Jesus. This is where many of us fall short.

We want so much from Christ BUT what are you giving back? Have you committed yourself to Him and His way of life or have you just come for the "good stuff?" Are you spending time with Him to learn how to live better, live a more fulfilled life, or just coming when the fire is hot, and you want a quick fix to your situations?

Let me share something about the quick fix...it will NEVER sustain you. It is your relationship with Christ that will get you through the most desperate times. If you have a relationship, rather than following for the moment, you have something to pull from when it seems like you are alone and need to figure out what to do. In that relationship, you can truly think about what He has shown you, what He has taught you, and what He has given you to pull through.

When the disciples were commissioned by Christ, He was able to send them FORWARD to spread the Gospel and make other disciples. He knew that they would be able to draw on what He had placed inside of them during their time together. Think about it, He was sending them FORWARD meanwhile the crowds that always just followed, you will note that He always sent them AWAY. They were sent back to the same place they were before they came in contact with Christ.

So, when it seems like you are in a state where you are constantly finding yourself BACK in the same situations, ask yourself...Am I a follower who comes to Christ in need, not wanting to stay with Him, seeking only what I need for the moment only to receive it and get sent back to the same condition or situation?

OR

Do I want to be a disciple? Am I one who will lay down all I thought I knew? Can I reconsider all I felt I needed or wanted, and walk with Christ? Am I ready to learn all I can from Him? Am I ready for a new way of life? Am I ready to build a relationship with Him, to gain ALL that I need to move FORWARD?

What choice will you make today? Will you dare to become a DISCIPLE?

Readings: Luke 6:17, Matthew 4:18-22

Reflections:

1. Are you following Jesus because of what He promised you or what you could receive from Him?
2. Are you a devoted disciple, putting aside time to spend with Him and to learn all that you possibly can?
3. What do you think is the difference between a fan follower and a disciple?
4. How do you compare with your differentiation?

DAY TWENTY-FOUR: WHAT DO YOU BELIEVE?

BELIEVE...such a simple word yet when put into action it becomes very complex.

On the eve of Resurrection Sunday, I cannot help but think of how there are many things we hear and see on a regular basis and chose to believe. Some of these things are very far-fetched yet, we believe. Someone can tell us fascinating story that seems a bit unbelievable, but we believe, even if the person is not trustworthy.

We believe the unthinkable and the unimaginable. We believe in studies performed by science, theories that have been in existence for hundreds of years although we never met the original scientist.

We believe in ghosts, witches, magic, the devil and that evil exist. Some even believe in angels, BUT when it comes to God and His Word, there is such UNBELIEF.

When it comes to believing that one day, His Son Jesus, was crucified then resurrected from death, somehow we cannot collectively believe.

We have belief in a lottery system that requires money spent to POSSIBLY be that one in a million who wins.

We believe what we read in the average book, yet never meeting the author but we believe what they wrote.

Somehow, we, in turn, cannot believe what is written in the Bible. Interestingly enough, we use the same reason we believe in other stories to NOT believe in the Bible. For example, it is said, that the Bible is written by man, therefore, giving reason to not believe but your science book was written by a man too.

There are many things written by a man that you believe in. The designs to create your chair you trust to hold you was done by man BUT you do not hesitate to sit on it. You believe it will hold you merely because it is there. You can give someone money to do a job that you believe they will do, even if you've never before met them.

What will it take to have that same belief in God? When will we start to put our trust in Him?

We CANNOT fathom the idea that in His infinite Glory and Power, we can receive miracles.

Maybe this is due to our failure to believe that God can do any and all things. Therefore, anything abnormal is "a miracle." When in fact, seeing the "miraculous" power of God should actually be a normal occurrence, BUT it is not because we fail to believe.

We have this need to understand everything to the point we will come up with any rationalization for it to make sense.

Let's look at the Theory of Evolution. What did it take for you to believe that man evolved from a creature, going through stages and metamorphosis, and finally became human walking upright, speaking multiple languages, and preserving and taking care of nature?

The question I have is, Why are these animals still not evolving into men?

Why are we giving birth to new life rather than continuing the process of evolution to populate the earth?

If we evolved from "creation" then who started the process of evolution causing this great transformation?

If you can believe that "something" caused the initial and finalization of transformation then why can you NOT believe that "something" caused creation? That God started creation.

If you can go through all the work to explain the big bang theory then why can you not believe in God that caused that thing to happen?

There is no better time than today to begin to change your thought process. To begin to challenge your personal reasoning.

Throughout the Gospels in the New Testament, you will find that Jesus performed over thirty-seven miracles. Interestingly enough, though so many miracles were performed, those who walked with him still stood in awe. I would dare to say that their awe was more of unbelief than simple amazement and joy.

They were so perplexed because despite calling Him, Lord, they really only saw Him in the flesh and not for who He truly was.

The disciples followed, listened, and watched Jesus. They even heard Him foretell of His own death and resurrection. When He appeared (after the resurrection), and the report was given to the disciples, they STILL DID NOT BELIEVE. It was not until He appeared before them and rebuked them did they believe. In fact, from the time they walked with Him through the resurrection, He rebuked them several times for their unbelief.

If anything, this should be a lesson to us. If those who have gone before us were witnesses yet rebuked for unbelief, then took the time to have their accounts recorded, then we should take them as lessons not to repeat rather than second-guessing them.

Why do we continue to be the perverse and faithless generation? Why must we see to believe instead of believing so we can see? The fact that we doubt is the very reason we do not nor cannot see great things happen. What if, instead, we changed our perspective? Changed our thought process and EXPECT first rather than doubt?

We spend time praying for things yet doubt until we see something happen. Some refuse to even pray because they do not believe anything different can or will happen. The Word of God says:

"Call to me and I will answer you, and will tell you great and hidden things that you have not known." (Jeremiah 33:3, NRSV)

The key here is to have an expectation. Know and understand who God is. In trying to rationalize who

Jesus is, you have to first STOP seeing Him simply as a man in the flesh. He was here in the flesh, BUT He was also here as THE SON OF GOD, leaving us with His Holy Spirit that guides us, and gives understanding and power. We can stop trying to figure out God on our own which leaves our natural mind in such unbelief. We need to move from unbelief to undeniable, unshakable, unmovable, unimaginable BELIEF.

As we dawn on a new day, thinking about the resurrection of Christ. Let's take Jesus off the cross and reflect upon the fact that HE defeated death. HE HAS RISEN. Since He rose again, we can know that NOTHING is impossible. Let tomorrow be your new beginning.

Look to see great things happen, no longer being comfortable in your doubt.

Pray and ask God for the unthinkable. Position yourself to receive, and allow the Promise of God to be fulfilled in your life and the life of those you love.

Stand and BELIEVE and watch God perform SIGNS and WONDERS before your very eyes.

> You are the God who performs miracles; you display your power among the peoples. (Psalm 77:14)

Reflections:

1. Do you need proof to believe?

2. What evidence has God already shown you that He exists and provides for you? What more do you need to see to believe in Him truly? Why do you need this?

3. Do you have the same difficulty believing in anything else? Why or Why not?

4. Why is it easier to believe in the things in the world than the things of God?

DAY TWENTY-FIVE: NEW BEGINNING

We often hear that you only get one chance …

One chance to make a first impression…

You get one chance at life, and there are no do-overs.

What if that were not entirely true?

What if you were given a second chance at life?

A second chance to live life to the fullest extent possible

Another chance to Love wholeheartedly

Another chance at freedom…another chance to be happy and full of hope and joy…

What if you looked back over your life and saw all that you wanted to accomplish or obtain but somehow did not, then, someone said, "It's not too late." Would you jump at the opportunity?

Let's put it to the test…

Today is a New Day
Today begins a new journey for the rest of your life
Today you got another chance at a new beginning…

NOW, WHAT?

Do not get stuck on thinking it is not possible because in Mark 10:27 Jesus said, "With man this is impossible, but not with God; all things are possible with God."

Now, we understand that He was talking about salvation and entering into the Kingdom of God but in this text, we also know that this is accomplished through God's Grace.

See, the grace of God extends unmerited mercy to us. Yes, something we have not worked for nor did anything to earn BUT He still does not want us to "fail" at this thing called life by getting stuck in our own way of doing things.

He is the God of another chance meaning He gives us opportunity after opportunity to get "it" right or get back on track. After all, every day, is a NEW DAY, right? It's a new beginning, an opportunity to see things differently than the day prior, an opportunity to make new choices/better choices, it is an opportunity to make changes and not get stuck in the "yesterday." Many in the Bible that started off making not so great choices and quite frankly, it displeased God, BUT that does not mean that He automatically gave up on them. Such a patient and merciful God, He saved those who formally did wrong against Him. Those that sought forgiveness were forgiven and given another chance.

Wow, He is a forgiving God too…Interesting. So, even when we are wrong and ask for forgiveness, He grants it? He just wipes that slate clean and gives us a fresh start….
Wonder how many of us would be so forgiving to those who have wronged us? Can we forgive as God forgives

us? What if reconciliation could save the life of another, would you or could you forgive so they could live?

God is willing to do it for you...He is willing to give you a FRESH START. An opportunity to CLEAN the SLATE, so that you can HAVE LIFE. Since He is willing to forgive you so that you may live, is it not befitting that you do the same for others? Shouldn't you forgive and let them live?

I want to leave you with these three thoughts:
1. Through God's Grace, you were able to awaken this morning. Not everyone was provided that chance to do so. You were provided with a new day to do something different and make different choices.

2. For anyone that has done wrong towards you, do as Christ commands us: FORGIVE. Remember, how can we NOT forgive our fellow brothers and sisters and expect to be forgiven, by God, for the things we do (or do not do)? In your forgiveness, the very life that you save may be your own.

3. Seek reconciliation with Christ. Allow Him to give you a new perspective on life. Seek Him and know that in Him you will find that "do over" that "other chance" that you never thought you would have because society says you only get one shot.

There is such a thing as a NEW BEGINNING. Isn't time for yours?

Reflections:

1. Treat today as if it is the start of a New Beginning. How are you going to start each day differently to obtain different results?
2. What are your new goals? What are the habits you are going to change? What old habits do you need to break? Are there new habits you need to start? Put them in your heart and mind then into practice.
3. Who can give you a fresh start to? Is there someone you need to forgive? Before moving forward with God, it is important to reconcile in your heart (and in person, if possible) with those you have an ought with.

STAGE VI: THE COVENANT

What does it mean to be in agreement with God

To Align yourself to His ways rather than leaning on your own understanding?

Insight comes from The Wisdom God gives but unless you KNOW Him, how can you know HIS voice and His Words?

DAY TWENTY-SIX: Be Still...

There is something to be said about how sharp senses become when one or more others become inoperable. For instance, when you are unable to see, you can hear more clearly. Let's look at Paul's journey to Damascus.

In Acts 9, we find Paul headed to Damascus on a journey seeking to find those who were following and spreading the good news of Jesus Christ. His mission was to find and "punish" them. Paul was one, in his own words, who was zealous for God. He was well-educated, and according to him, based on what he was taught and believed, he was doing the right thing. Unfortunately, at times the very thing we have been taught and operate in can also cause one to become stagnate if we are not careful or mindful of what is happening around us.

What do I mean by this?

Simply put, we should never get so comfortable in our knowledge that we cannot see and miss a move of God. Here, Jesus came, and there was a massive move yet, Paul could not see what was happening.

So, here is another way of looking at what happened on his journey.

In Acts 22: 7-11, Paul says, "While I was on my way and approaching Damascus, about noon a great light from heaven suddenly shone about me.7 I fell to the ground and heard a voice saying to me, 'Saul, Saul, why are you persecuting me?' 8 I answered, 'Who are you, Lord?' Then he said to me, 'I am Jesus of Nazareth whom you are persecuting.' 9 Now those who were with me saw the light but did not hear the voice of the one who was speaking to me. 10 I asked, 'What am I to do, Lord?' The Lord said to me, 'Get up and go to Damascus; there you will be told everything that has been assigned to you to do.' 11 Since I could not see because of the brightness of that light, those who were with me took my hand and led me to Damascus." (NRSV)

Here we see the following:
1. Blinded by the light, Paul could clearly hear the LORD's voice and His directions.
2. Now in a position where he must be humbled enough to follow the lead of someone else
3. In Damascus, he had to WAIT on the help the LORD sent him rather than doing things his own way. His original plan and way are now interrupted.
4. The help the Lord sent Paul, well... it was an unlikely source. The help was part of the very sect of people he sought to capture and bring to "punish." The very same people he KNEW were wrong but were truly following Christ. The Lord sent a disciple to restore Paul's sight, baptize him, and provide him his instructions for his assignment from the Lord.

Sometimes we make the mistake of believing so much that we are always right about everything...believing we are living righteous yet we are really leaning toward self-righteousness.
In this state, it is easy to find yourself on the opposite side of God:
Failing to hear appropriately...having impaired vision...missing a move of God.

Let's make sure we are following the Lord's voice and directions and not our own. What is the best way to make sure we hear clearly?

1. Block out everything we "see." Without focusing on everything that we think we know, we can actually heighten our sense of hearing.
2. Turn off all the calamity around us that drowns out the small still voice. Maybe you need to, steal away and find a quiet place away from all the noise and chaos.
3. BE STILL...stop moving so much. You cannot be busy with everything and listen to the only thing that really matters.

Sometimes you just have to be still and close your eyes to hear clearly...to receive new vision...to really understand His word.
BE STILL: Stop ALL movement
Know that I AM God: Acknowledge His plan and surrender to it

Reflections:

1. Practice being still and just listening. Sit in a quiet place, no distractions, close your eyes, relax, and just listen. What did you hear? What did you see?
2. Spend time daily, listening for the small still voice. The more you spend time listening, the more you will hear. Always write what you hear and experience.

DAY TWENTY-SEVEN: ARE WE ONE BODY?

"The most segregated hour in Christian America is 11 o'clock on Sunday morning."

In this day and age, this divide still exists. It is the most appalling as we use terms like "contemporary Christian Music" or "Black Gospel Music" rather than using a word to describe what should be...WORSHIP or SONGS of WORSHIP AND PRAISE.
We say we believe in God, but we are also divided over doctrine, worship, how to worship, tradition, and dare I say...RELIGION.
Everyone is right, and others are wrong, which actually makes us ALL wrong in thinking that one is superior to another. Are we not wrong for taking the position that one is higher than the next...that we are without fault...without blemish...without spot or wrinkle? I understand that is what we should STRIVE for BUT honestly, NO ONE has ARRIVED. I mean, if we are walking around thinking we have ARRIVED, isn't that a sin in itself...being SELF RIGHTEOUS?
We have become so divided as Christians that it is not a wonder that the enemy continues to come in and attack over and over and over.
How can a divided kingdom stand? How can we win or overcome when we are always fighting each other? How can we overcome anything when we are constantly focused on putting down another's house rather than finding ways to work together? Shouldn't we BE the example for the world in which we live?

Living in Love
Working in Love
Operating in Love

While Christ was in the flesh, walking the earth, those who were so "educated" in the scriptures and in the law thought they knew so much that any and every time Jesus did anything or spoke, they challenged Him. When He healed people and cast out demons, and the Pharisees and Sadducees did not understand, they tried to call Him the very thing He was casting out.

They challenged Him even on the Law, but in all they thought they understood, Christ proved they truly had no real REVELATION to those things which were given to Moses.

If Jesus did anything "contrary" to their "customs/traditions" they attempted to rebuke Him. In an attempt to PRESERVE what they believed to understand, to uphold their RELIGION and TRADITION, they sought to kill Him and those who have a relationship with Him.

Don't you know that no matter what, the relationship you have with Jesus is something that cannot be killed by someone else? Even in Spirit, our relationship with Christ continues.

When it feels like the world is suffering and fading away, it is our relationship with Christ that lives on. Through our relationship with Him and operating in the Spirit (His Spirit), we should be able to lay aside tradition and religion in times of "war" when we as Christians are needed the most.

This is not the time for a war between Christians BUT a war Among Christians standing together to fight the battle between Good and EVIL. We must stand united...together against the enemy and his ways...his tactics, and his army.

We should genuinely be THE ARMY OF THE LORD, UNITED IN BATTLE, PROCLAIMING VICTORY FOR THE KINGDOM
Let's not be the very thing that sought to kill Christ - Religion and SELF Righteousness
Remember:
THE CHURCH is more than the four walls you enter into on Sunday mornings.
The BODY of CHRIST MUST LEARN to OPERATE in UNITY. We cannot afford to be segregated.
We must LIFT up each other, not tear each other down.

How else will the world start looking at us differently?

Reflections:

1. What is the difference between righteousness and self-righteousness.?
2. Which characteristics do you exhibit?
3. Sometimes we can learn from others. Have you seen others who are righteous or self-righteous?
4. Examine what areas you need to change or adjust.

DAY TWENTY-EIGHT: THE RIVER

"Teacher, Teacher," the man cried as he ran into the building.
"What is it," the teacher replied
"I just saw something amazing," the man exclaimed
"What did you see," asked the teacher.
"A woman is sitting on the bank of the river," the student said with much excitement.

"Why do you find this so amazing," asked the teacher.

"Because this river has been dry for so long and now there is so much water there," the man answered, not understanding the lack of excitement from his teacher.

"Well, should not a river contain water," the teacher asked.

"Yes, teacher, but what was the source of the water? The land is dry for it has not rained in such a long time."

The man sat as the teacher began to speak.

This river that you speak of was a dry and deserted place, but it was not always that way. For long ago, it was a beautiful area. This was a place where people would come to rejoice, relax, find revitalization...to be refreshed.
They would come and fish in an area, and the supply of fish was never lacking.

But the people who enjoyed this place so much did nothing to preserve the area. In fact, they would leave behind their trash rather than clean the area. They cared not about the water where they were refreshed and received food from.

They tossed all the things they did not want into the water, polluting the river.

When other people would pass by this place and saw how unkept it was, they assumed this must be a dumping ground. So, that is what it eventually became.

Such an unsightly place, the people stopped coming. Eventually, the trash blocked the flow of water. The once free-flowing river has now dried up.

Before the teacher could continue, the man asked, "But how did the water come back to such an unclean and dry place?"

The teacher continued...

Recently migrants came through the area. They had been traveling for so long and from so far away, for they were looking for a place to escape from where they previously were. They were seeking a place of refuge. They wanted a new home, a place of freedom. When they reached the bank of which they did not know was previously a river, the people decided they would travel just a little further and rest on the other side.

They walked down into the dry river. Their trek across the barren land, full of things thrown away and shattered glass, began.

They lugged all they had, which was not much and pressed their way through stepping on the broken glass and cutting their feet.

Oh, the pain they felt and the blood that came but if

they could just get to the other side.
When they did, they immediately stopped for their feet were so cut and bruised they could not bear to walk any further. They collapsed on the other side of the bank.
As they began to pull the pieces of glass from their blood covered feet, they cried out, and tears began to fall.
Helping one another, more tears fell.
Seeing the pain in each other's face...more tears fell.

There were tears of pain
Tears of sorrow
Tears of mourning
Tears of empathy
Tears of love for one another
And Tears of Relief

"Teacher, that is such a beautiful story but where has the water come from?"

"The tears child...the tears replenished the water BUT did you not notice the NEW LOCATION of the water?

Your eyes are thinking it is amazing because you just see the same old place with a little water.
But, the woman you saw...she comes there and sits every morning. She finds rest and peace at the new place that was created.

The area was always meant to be a resting place but the old people, on the other side, took it for granted.
The new people had to go through so much for their new place of peace.
Through blood, sweat, and tears, they have a place to sit and reflect on how they made it through. They can

Fresh Manna: Journey To A New Beginning

reflect on how they made it over to the other side.

They see the beauty of it all. The NEW RIVER with the sun shining and reflecting off the water.
But just on the other side...the edge of the land...an outer bank is a reminder of what they conquered.
They continue to rejoice here.
Their times of reflection and rejoicing brings great tears of overwhelming JOY that continue to daily replenish the water.

"Now," asked the teacher, "Do you see, do you understand what you should really be amazed at?"

Reflections:

1. What was the lesson the teacher wanted the student to see and understand?
2. As you read today, what did you notice in the story? What stood out? Why?

DAY TWENTY-NINE: THE RIVER...part II

As the days continued on, the man continued his daily walks to go meet with the teacher, in the building. It was so enlightening, the things he learned as they sat and talked. On this particular morning, something was different.

As he began his walk towards the temple, suddenly he felt a strong quake and saw things shift from their usual state.

He moved quickly towards the building as he anticipated talking to the teacher about this sudden shift.

He ran to the building, but the teacher was not there. He went out searching then noticed something unusual.

There was a crowd gathered ahead at the bank of the water and before them were three springs coming up from the standing water.

The crowd was standing at first, in amazement, then as they fell to their knees, the man could not believe what he now saw.

"T E A C H E R," he exclaimed almost slowly as if he was crying out the name.

Once closer, he cried as he too fell to his knees, "What's happening?
Why are you here amongst the people and not away inside? Why have you come here? To this place?"

Fresh Manna: Journey To A New Beginning

"I went to the temple to find you, and you were not there."

"Come, my son. Let me show you," the teacher began to speak as he picked up the man.

Every day, I sat in the temple. It was a beautiful place where people would gather to pray. They came with a desire to learn, gain understanding, and to be fed. It was a sacred place. They would love one another, always helping one another for they were one family. But then everyone wanted their own family. All were leaders in their own way, yet no one wanted to listen. They forgot I was the TRUE TEACHER.

Slowly, they went from paying homage to Me, to desiring it for themselves. The family began to break apart. The youngest, of them all, were left to suffer, but they were innocent. I cared for them still and continued to feed them while others were oblivious to what was going on.

Eventually, I begin to send them forth to spread what they learned. These were the ones I could trust to go and help those who were displaced. They were sent to find the migrants and direct them to Me. They were unafraid to do what I commissioned them to do, and they knew the work was not about them but about My plan.

Meanwhile, the others who were busy doing their own work, and focused on their own agenda, were also the same ones who desecrated the water and land before it. I waited every day in that place, hoping, waiting, and desiring for them to return home but they did not.

Fresh Manna: Journey To A New Beginning

I sent for them over and over and over, but they would not receive My messengers.

These here, they knew not of the once beautiful temple, but they heard stories of the rumblings that carried on there. They vowed never to enter into such a place for it was no better than where they were and from where they attempting to escape. They still, every day, continued to make their way towards Me regardless of what they had to endure.

They took care of each other although none of them had much of anything to give. They, unsure, what it meant to really know I was there, knew that they must love one another for nothing is greater than love. And when they made it to the resting place they heard so much about from the messengers, they "reflected" daily and was full of gratitude.

"But why have you come here, teacher," the man asked. "It's not safe, did you not feel the earth quake earlier? Everything moved. And the springs that shot up and still flowing strongly…what was going on, I do not understand. Are you angry? What is happening?" The man tried to be calm, but it was all just so overwhelming.

My son, My son…settle yourself. Peace is here in the place.

Yes, you felt the earth quake as I began to move from the old place to the new. In the shift, nothing can stay the way in which it was before. It is time for a change. The time has come that I must show myself to the people.

The people who have longed for me and I have longed for them. They thought they were forgotten about and beginning to lose all hope, but they must know I have never forgotten them.

And now, in a humble and grateful condition, they yet yearn for so much more. They have thirst for so long, BUT today, WE have formed a new covenant. Things as you once knew them shall be no more for I am doing a NEW THING.

These THREE springs are a reminder that WE are here and they shall thirst no more but shall stay refreshed.

If you look closely in the third spring, you shall see what they saw...The RAINBOW that belongs to Me to remind the people of the covenant and the promise.

These are my children, and I AM forever with them.

This they know in their hearts and have paid homage.

Reflections:

1. What did you notice? What questions did you have while reading?
2. After reading, sit still and listen. Record what you hearing or feeling?

DAY THIRTY: THE RAIN

Now, time had passed yet the man continued to meet with the teacher for their scheduled lessons and talks although they no longer met inside the old building. Most times they walked openly together where others would see them as they would pass by.

This particular morning, the man asked questions that had been on his mind for a few days. You see, it had been raining for days now, but the people around seemed not to be phased by the rain. Well, at least not in a negative way. In fact, most times he saw them, they were out rejoicing in the rain. He thought they were being foolish and decided to talk with his teacher about this "foolishness."

"Teacher?"

"Yes, son."

"I've noticed lately that, for starters, it has been raining for some time now and honestly, I'm pretty tired of it. When will the sunshine? The rain just makes it soaking wet. We cannot do much when it is always raining. And have you seen the people?"

"What about them," the teacher asked.

"You do not see them dancing around in the rain? What is wrong with them? Can they not see the mess the rain is making? Yet, they dance around looking like fools."

"You should not mock things that you do not

understand," the teacher quickly responded.

Confused, the man asked, "What do you mean?"

The teacher spoke:

You appear to believe that you know what is best. You assume you know that during this time, it is better for the sun to shine than it is for the rain to fall.

You assume that you know the most about the rain, when in fact, your vision is obscured.

Each day you walk here to meet with Me. You walk by the people, yet, only take notice of things that you believe they are doing wrong, things improper, or strange. Yet, you took no notice of all the times you passed by and they were out in the "fields" sowing.

"Sowing," the man asked.

Yes, sowing! Planting seeds, the teacher continued.

So, now, that the rain has come, they are rejoicing for the harvest that will eventually follow. They understand that the land will be plenished with new life…trees, plants, and vines, that will bring forth "fruit."

Within each is more seeds they will continue to give back…to sow, rather than tossing them away. They will again reap the benefits of the harvests that will continue to follow.

The rain is a nuisance only to those who have sown nothing, therefore expect nothing.

Pondering on what he just heard, the man finally spoke, "I have never thought of it that way." After moments of silence, he spoke again.

"Teacher?"

"Yes."

"I understand about the rain, but what about the storms?"

"What about them?"

"Should the people be concerned about the storms? Even in the middle of the storm, they continued to dance as if nothing was happening."

The teacher answered:

These people understand that with the rain, storms will almost certainly pass through. More importantly, they understand that storms will come and go. They choose to rejoice, knowing that this too shall pass and refuse to be distracted by focusing on the storm. They also understand that just as the storm will keep moving and pass over them, it is important to stay in place and NOT follow the storm.

If they follow the storm, then they will move out of place and no longer in a position to receive the harvest.

Fresh Manna: Journey To A New Beginning

Lesson:

Dance in the rain, rejoicing for the harvest will soon follow. Never get distracted by the storms as they shall pass. Do not make the mistake of following the moving storm system as you will find yourself in a place where you miss your harvest. Don't let your hard work go to waste because you got distracted. hell never wants you to receive what Heaven has been preparing for you.

Reflections:

1. Do you find the rain in your life a nuisance or a blessing?
2. Review your reflections from days 28-30. What did you collectively notice?

STAGE VII: I AM HERE

Worlds Apart, He whispers to me while I walk on the road. The sun at my back and the wind against my face. I walk alone, but yet I'm not really alone for He is letting me know that He is here.

"I hear you," I respond out of the depths of my heart.

"My child, look ahead what do you see?"

"A mountain," I respond.

"No, look again," He says.

"A hill," I say as I continue to walk further along.

Then there is silence, and the wind stops as I continue to walk alone but not alone. I hear again, the whisper. I feel the wind again.

"I'm here," I say.

"My child," HE says, "What do you see?"

I'm looking ahead, but I see nothing. "Where did the mountain go," I asked.

"How could you forget that fast," He says. "That tiny pebble you kicked to the side, off of your path just a few steps back. Do you not recall?"

"Yes," I answered.

"That was your mountain you saw so great at the beginning. As you went further along, You knew I was with you. Knowing that I placed you there, the mountain became smaller and smaller. By the time you approached it, I made it so small that without realizing it, you kicked it out of your way. It became non-existent! This is what happens when you trust Me and My Word," He says.

"Stay the course for nothing is greater, bigger, nor more powerful than I. You need not worry when you stay on the path on which I have placed you. Nothing will get in the way or stop you from where I am taking you….Just stay with Me."

"I AM here!"

DAY THIRTY-ONE: ALIVE WITH CHRIST

I am not waiting to die to live with God

I am living with God now

In my heart, I am living with God

I can carry Him with me in everywhere I go and everything I do

I AM ALIVE because He is ALIVE in me

So many are awaiting the day they can be with Jesus but tell me why can you not be with Him now? What is stopping you from being with Him now?

We are waiting to die so we can be with Him

We say, "in that glorious day when we all see Jesus..." but why wait?

Let your flesh come under submission so you can be with Him NOW and have a NEW LIFE. Align yourself with Him rather than trying to live on your own.

For if you are always still doing things that are pleasing to you and for you only, then your FLESH is very much still alive, and your soul must be revived.

If you have given your life to Christ and living for Him then, your soul has been resurrected...once again ALIVE...walking, living, breathing with Him.

My thoughts are His thoughts

My beliefs are His beliefs

My heart beats for those things His heart longs and beats for

I breathe because He breathes through me

I see as He sees and my vision is no longer obscured and distorted

I love as He loves and I hate as He hates

My life is no longer my own as I am wrapped up in His designed purpose and destiny

I no longer have to wait for the glorious day when I die, go to heaven and see Jesus for I have allowed myself to die NOW.

I am born again in Him

I live with Him now and every moment of every day of my life

I am alive with Christ and have found my heaven

I live in peace

I live in wealth

I live in prosperity

I live in good health

I live in love

I sing His praises

He has allowed me to entered into His gates and I sing with the angels and worship Him

I am with Him, and He is with me, even while I walk on this earth.

Reflections:

1. How can you live with Christ now?
2. What does it mean to you, to be alive with Christ?
3. What does it mean, to you, to be Free with Christ?
4. What does it mean to Have peace with Christ?

DAY THIRTY-TWO: STAY HUMBLE

It is interesting how many people who started out doing great things, lost their way when their focus changed. They shifted from what they needed or were required to do, to a selfish need for the spotlight, for massive attention, platforms, celebrity status, recognition, center stage, etc.

Truth is...

What you are doing in your everyday life is really no comparison to the sacrifice Christ made. All the time He walked the earth, even He either mentioned or reminded others that He was doing the work of His Father and gave honor to God. Surely, we are not greater than He is.

At the end of the day, we MUST learn to just get over ourselves. It was all about God in the first place. All the credit, all the honor goes to Him.

We must learn to be thankful, give honor and stay humble.

Selah

Father, I pray that in all things we remember that you are the First, The Last, The Beginning and The End. We can do NOTHING without you, and we are NOTHING without you. I pray that in all that we do we remember to first give thanks to you, always honoring you. I pray that in all that you give us, show us, and take us, we remember that had it not been for you, we would not be here and in all these things we remain humble. Father, I pray that in all our work, others will see more of you than they will ever see of us so that you shall always be glorified for the focus should be and must be about you. For each and every day that we live for you, others will want to know the Great God that we serve and have a desire to serve you and have a relationship with you as well, and in the end, we shall be blessed. For this is what you desire. Amen

Reflections: *(What's really in your heart)*

1. What do you desire more than anything in the world? Why? What would you do once you receive it?
2. The very thing you desire, it is for yourself, for others, or for God?
3. How have you accomplished or obtained the things you have?
4. Can you give without expecting something in return? What if you never received a "thank you" could you still continue to give or serve?
5. How do your answers compare with today's devotion? Do they reflect humility, pride, or selfishness? What changes must you make to reflect godly characteristics of selflessness and humility?

DAY THIRTY-THREE: WHY, GOD?

Recently, I was on Facebook and noticed a post about Christian accountability that was meant to be enlightening yet also humorous. This ended up turning into an interesting discussion about God and His willingness to allow things to happen in this world that troubles us.

What I find most interesting is that later responses to the post were a complete miss to the underlying message. Here, let me share a little:

"If God is so good and loving, why does he allow so much evil in the world?"

The Christian says, "When you see Him, why don't you ask?"

The atheist says, "Wouldn't you want to ask him?"

The Christian replied, "I wouldn't dare. I'd be afraid. He would ask me the same question."

The first response:

"Because God doesn't control man. He allows us to have free will. As a result, bad crap happens. We either make poor choices, or others do, which affects others within the universe. We are not God's puppets. Although, it seems so easy to blame God and lay all evil as his fault. Unfortunately, free will allows for mistakes and intentions of others to put ripples in the universal flow of right and wrong. Sooner or later, those ripples affect us all."

Decent response, right? There is some self-accountability there as well as helping us to understand that we all have a part to play. Gives you much to think about, IF you are willing to sit and really think. Sometimes, we are unable to do that. Sometimes, we just get a little stuck on, "...so much evil in the world." Some of us get to that place, and it becomes that "sunken place" where even if there are things that happen you do not understand, that feeling turns to misplaced anger.

Here, let's take a look at this response

"I disagree. If God allows free will. Then he favors evil. The Woman who is raped, the child who is abused. What about their free will? It is said the God is omnipresent. That means Gods is right there, watching murder, Rape, Child abuse, watched genocide, Slavery, Atrocities without count. Every child in Nazi Germany who was experimented on. God was in the room, doing nothing. Oh, That's Right Free will! People who are murdered, but not saved, yet the murder can repent and be saved, the victim, burns in hell, and who just stand by doing nothing? If God stopped the free will of the murderer like he did Pharaoh so that he would not let the people go, just so that God could show off. How was that free will? How is this free will, when not one of us asked to be brought into existence? He who is Omni-Knowledgeable, knows everything in advance, before creation. Yet make not one adjustment, go right on ahead, creates Billions and Billions of people who will burn in hell till time runs out. That is not free will. The Tree of the Knowledge of Good and Evil could have been placed on top of a Mountain. But No it was placed smack dab in the center of the Garden and was pointed

out. No, that is entrapment. Like a Bait car."

This was my unfavorable response:

So, did you have free will when you responded to this post or were you controlled in some form or another? Do you have the choice to believe in God or not? Do you have a choice to believe and worship any way you choose? Considering that no one is perfect in this world, can you say you are the exemption and have done nothing wrong or bad in your life? We love to jump to the worse things like murder as examples, but, for the sake of argument let's just keep it overly simple...During even your childhood (teenage years included) was there ever a time where you did something your parents said NOT to do but you did it anyway? As a result, you had to deal with the consequences of your actions? Well, if so, you made a choice. The choice was you would rather do what you wanted or give in to something or even give in to someone else and deal with the consequences. Maybe not realizing the consequences until much later. Seems like an oversimplified metaphor but it really is that simple. The problem is 1. Many times there is such a lack of understanding that we overreach and blame. 2. Have a lack of faith or put our faith in the wrong things. 3. Because we as humans want to be able to have a finite answer to everything, we get upset when we don't, therefore, focusing our anger on the wrong things

While I am in no way stating that feelings, such as unfairness or anger, about something are wrong, I do believe that sometimes when we do not understand why someone did something to us, we immediately "curse" God. We look at everything as being His fault. Yes, we really do have free will...we really do have choices and the decisions we make actually affect others. Yes, there are other circumstances in which absolutely nothing will make sense. Those can be the most disturbing. The truth is, it is ok to be disturbed by things we naturally see. I am sure that God does not expect us to walk around untouched by anything but even with all of our emotions, we have to be wise enough to know, accept, and understand that we are NOT knowledgeable of everything. Since we all not all-knowing, then the outcome of certain situations are rightfully upsetting.

We are humans, and we want answers. We feel that we are owed answers to every situation, all the time but what if you were actually given an answer, would you really be satisfied? Would you relinquish all of your emotions? What if the answer you received was not the answer you expected? What happens then? Think of how we responded to situations as children:

You wanted to obtain or to do something, but your parents told you, "NO!" That's it, nothing more. What's the first response, "Why?" Right? This is not to say that a heinous crime is the same as your desire to have you way as a child, but this is just putting it in the a basic and relatable way.

Ok, moving along...

Now, whatever response you received from your parents just was never the "RIGHT" answer. Nothing would have satisfied you other than having things your way. At that moment, your parents are the absolute worst people ever, right? And guess what, they knew that with time, you would be ok? They understood that there were just some things you would just never really understand and nothing would change that.

What happens when we fast forward a decade (or more)? Are we still having the same responses after rightful cries of, "Why, God?" OR have we throughout the years continued also to seek wisdom? With that wisdom, we know that it is ok to feel but just as important, we learn that:

1. True wisdom helps you understand that satisfaction has nothing to do with getting the answer that you want.
2. True wisdom helps you understand that it is ok to not have all or any of the answers.
3. True wisdom helps you understand that sometimes, you just will not understand.

"If any of you is lacking in wisdom, ask God, who gives to all generously and ungrudgingly, and it will be given you. But ask in faith, never doubting, for the one who doubts is like a wave of the sea, driven and tossed by the wind; for the doubter, being double-minded and unstable in every way, must not expect to receive anything from the Lord." (James 1:5-8, NRSV)

Remember:
He who thinks he knows it all is not smart;
He who accepts that he doesn't is NOT foolish.
Do NOT be a know it all fool; Seek Wisdom

Fresh Manna: Journey To A New Beginning
True Wisdom comes but only from God

Reflections:

1. Can you relate to the sentiments of the original response? Are there things you hold against God because you need answers or do not understand?
2. Are the things you seek answers to keeping you from establishing a deeper relationship with God?
3. What answers could God or a man give to satisfy you and help you move forward? Would any answer really make things better?
4. Can you accept lack of understanding as answer if you knew it would also bring you peace of mind?
5. What is more important, answers to never ending questions about things beyond your control or peace of mind?

DAY THIRTY-FOUR: ACTION VS. WORDS

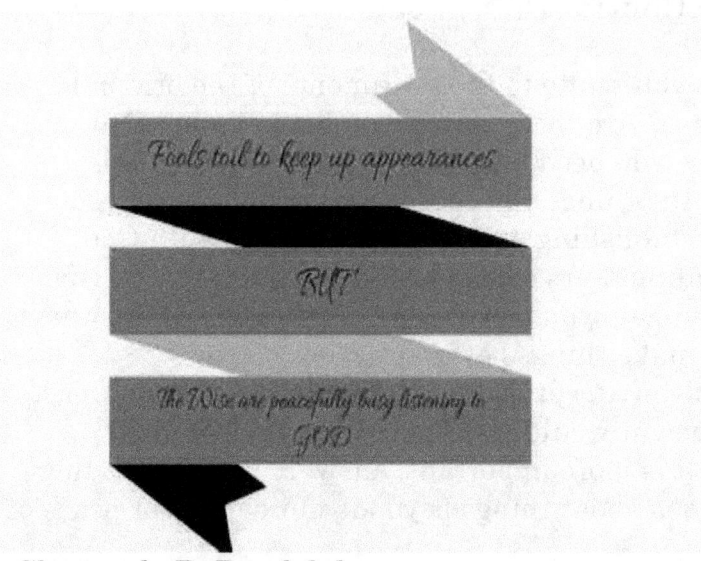

- Shawanda R. Randolph

Do your actions speak contrary to who you claim to be?

This relates to the common phrase, "actions speak louder than words."

Though we would usually apply this when someone has done something wrong to us, yet says, "I love you" or "I'm sorry." We would quickly toss out, " Actions speak louder than words," like a sharp dagger to make a cut that hurts just as much as we were previously affected. We would attempt to drive the point home by saying anything you want, but it is what you do that really matters.

In this instance, let's take a different approach to the same words. Let's use them in response to who we say we are.

Many of us claim to be something or someone, yet our actions speak contrary to our self-proclaimed titles, positions, or roles.

To keep it simple, let's reflect on the example of the role of a student.

A parent sends their child to school every day prepared to learn. In parent's mind, the child is in school as a student, BUT when the report card comes home, it presents a different result.

The parent discovers the child's grades are sub-par. The child has demonstrated misconduct and paid no attention to the taught lessons. In fact, the student cannot recall what he was taught nor can he give an account of what he was really doing during his time in school.

Now, was this child really a student or was he just going to school?

For those who state the child was still a student, this may very well explain some of the problems we see with adults in their roles...failure to see the TRUE characteristics of a particular role, accept those responsibilities, and be held accountable for their actions.

If I have gone to school with intentions other than

learning all I can from whoever was responsible for teaching me...

If I fail to pay attention...

If I spend more time talking than listening...I may not be a student despite the fact that people think I am because of what I have said. Eventually, the report will come out, telling or exposing everything.

Going a step further...

The Teacher: Who are you teaching?

What are you teaching?

Are you spending enough time in preparation to teach or winging it?

What are you studying

What does your day consist of

Are you spending only 10% of your time dedicated to those things related to teaching, learning or preparing to teach?

If this is you, then are you REALLY a teacher or fake, a phony, an imposter, impersonator?

You can use the same and apply to it any position: ministers, caregivers, leaders, Christians, "people of faith," husbands, wives, mothers, fathers, sisters, brothers, family, friends...the list goes on and on and on...

We all have a place we should be...a role to play but what is yours? Are you fulfilling your right role? Have you taken the right actions in your role or have you been slacking, been out of place and not living up to those responsibilities?

My mom would always say something that we hated to hear as children, but we laugh, appreciate, and repeat it now as adults.

She says: "If it doesn't come out in the wash, it will come out in the rinse."

So, as it applies to who we are, claim to be and our actions, it will all come out at some point. We will all get exposed for who we really are: A FAKER OR A MAKER

One faking their way or making things happen

Accountability is REAL. Are you able, ready, and willing to give account for your actions when the report is read?

If you are going to stake claim to being a particular type of person, then take the time to ensure your actions are an accurate representation of who you say you are.

Anyone can ACT the part. Masks are real, but it takes dedication, commitment, drive, motivation, ambition, skill, knowledge, understanding and WISDOM to be who you NEED to be.

Reflections:

1. Who have you claimed to be? A friend, student, Christian, etc.?
2. Define the role and responsibility and characteristics of this person? Ask others for their definition.
3. Do you fit the definition? Would others agree?
4. Challenge yourself and ask those in your life if you have demonstrated, to them, who you thought you were to them. Learn how to be a better friend, parent, child, relative, neighbor, student, Christian, worker, leader, etc.

DAY THIRTY-FIVE: BEWARE OF THE PUFFERFISH

A PUFFER FISH?

REALLY?! Yes, A Pufferfish.

Recently, there was a video that went viral on social media about a puffer fish. The video, originally part of a broadcast that aired on BBC, showcased this species and the great work it does to attract the opposite sex. In this case, let's just focus on how it worked to bring attention to itself.

The fish worked countless hours, ultimately creating this "masterpiece" in the ground/sand. Such a beautiful intricate design it created with its fins. Upon completion, the narrator talks about how unique this is and if this does not bring him (the fish) attention than NOTHING will.

Wow! All of that work and such beauty created and for what?

Just to get attention? Just to draw attention to the puffer fish? The same species that is also known to:

- Be Foul tasting
- Carry a toxin that is deadly to humans

Did you know that the toxin of a puffer fish is more poisonous than cyanide? There is enough toxin in ONE fish to kill THIRTY humans, AND there is NO known antidote.

I know…I know this same fish is edible YET there are dangers in being untrained or unskilled in handling such fish and preparing for consumption. Why? Because if not handled correctly, the result could be the end of someone's life.

Why is all of this important?

Because many of us tend to walk around in life, failing to pay attention to what is happening around us.

We are blinded by the pretty things

We are blinded by emotional things and therefore becoming weak and vulnerable.

We fail to see the dangers of the "puffer fish." We only see the beautiful masterpiece he created not realizing it was solely created to "draw" us in.

And once we took part in what the puffer fish had to offer, it would surely kill us.

Do not be deceived by those who attempt to appeal to your senses, your desires, or even your ego. These people will create a façade to make you think that what they have is so great when in fact, your connection to them is deadly.

Connecting to the wrong people will kill your present and most certainly your future. The dreams you had, the work you have been accomplishing, gone…over in an instant.

In Judges 16, The story of Samson and Delilah, Samson is a judge and Nazarite whom God had given supernatural strength to.

Having to overcome much and prevailing in his life ultimately becoming a judge for over 20 years.

In Judges 16 He began to give in to temptation and eventually would cost him his life.

Already starting his fall, he was attracted to, fell in love with, and married a woman that he was NEVER supposed to connect with. This attraction had much to do with an established weakness. In fact, his enemy was able to use this weakness against him by getting his wife to 'COAX' him into revealing the source of his strength. His wife knew the justification for identifying this source was so the Philistines could overpower (and take) Samson.

Three times, his wife did exactly what was asked of her. Those three times, she asked her husband what made him so strong. Each time she received an answer, she attempted to use that against him to help the enemy overtake her husband.
When the initial attempts did not work, she appealed to her husband, expressing how he "mocked" her and lied to her.

Now, let's think here...

1. His wife has now, asked what makes his strength great and how he could be bound.

2. Samson tells her something, and she has now bound him on 2 occasions with bowstrings/ropes and woven his locks, hoped this worked, tested him by yelling that the Philistines were present.
3. When each attempt failed, she "cries" you mocked and lied to me in hopes that Sampson would now tell the truth.

Listen, at this point, anyone who is in their RIGHT mind would have put an end to this foolishness. Unfortunately, when we need to feed or fill an empty space/void in our lives, we allow that space to get filled with the wrong people and the wrong things. No matter what happens, no matter what they do, that thing is just so "pretty" or mesmerizing that we keep it or them around.

Moving on…

Finally, after the third time, Delilah, appeals to him by saying "How could you say I love you when your heart is not with me?" She has now done major work to draw Samson in. Tired and unable to withstand the nagging, Sampson gives in. He REVEALS the source of his strength and tells how he can become overpowered.

Wasting no time, Delilah works with the enemy to "go in for the kill."

It is ALL downhill from here. The Lord leaves Sampson. He is seized, blinded, and imprisoned by his enemy.

Fresh Manna: Journey To A New Beginning

Eventually, Samson's locks grew back, but he was still among his enemies. It was only by God's mercy that he was given his strength ONE LAST TIME, to allow revenge upon his enemies BUT it is just as important to note that when these Philistines died, Sampson, died along with them.
He died along with those who lured, captured, blinded and imprisoned him.

What does this all have to do with the puffer fish?

Well, when you are lured in and partake of the pufferfish's toxins, your body goes through stages leading to death.

It is relatively similar to what we saw happen to Samson.

The moment you consume tainted pufferfish, the tetrodotoxin poison goes to work on turning off the switch that is your life.

1. The nervous system is immediately attacked, preventing your neurons from communicating with each other and your brain. The toxin stops your muscles from functioning. This means that you STOP thinking correctly and are unable to respond or react to situations appropriately.

2. You feel it on your tongue as neurotransmitters stop working. Much like the enemy appealing to your senses. he helps to change your appetite. You are now unable to withstand the sensation for offensive things. You are unable to tell what is good or bad for you.

3. You begin to feel dizzy, experience nausea, headaches, and vomiting. Your body is in trouble. When you vomit, your body is unable to keep down things it needs. Your body begins to REJECT things that will adequately sustain you.

4. You experience difficulty breathing along with a loss of autonomic functions (heart rate, digestion, etc.). The heart stops functioning correctly much like it does when we disconnect from God. The heart turns toward things that will not bring life but rather cut you off from the SOURCE of Life.

5. You become totally paralyzed. You are conscious but unable to fight off any attacks.

You are bound to DIE

We must really begin to search our hearts. It is here that the enemy sees what our true desires are and tries to appeal to them. Once he does, he sends in the pufferfish to dress everything up, make it look beautiful...perfect, or like just what you "need."

We cannot be so vulnerable to fall into these traps. We must stay on guard for if we do not, we get lured into the lair of the pufferfish who will release its toxins to take us out.

Reflections: *(Know your vices, so you are aware of how you can fall for traps.)*

1. This question is being asked of you again. What do you want more than anything in the world? Why?
2. What draws you to the things you desire most? Do you desire, fame, fortune, popularity, honor, respect, to simply noticed?
3. What do you get from doing for others?
4. What makes you vulnerable? What are your weaknesses? How can you avoid weaknesses while you are working to become stronger?

Fresh Manna: Journey To A New Beginning

STAGE VIII: SIDE WITH PEACE

Whom you decide to rest your loyalties with shall determine the outcome of your state of mind.

For alignment with God shall bring you TRUE PEACE no matter who tries to stand against you.

Knowing that you have moved/done things according to what God has instructed, then you should have PEACE

No man can destroy the PERFECT PEACE given by God

The PERFECT PEACE that comes from a TRUE COVENANT with God.

As we draw closer to God, we should begin to care about the things and people He cares about. We try to see the world through the lenses of others and God. We begin to shift focus from ourselves as we grow, and focus on others in need.

During your final stage of this journey, you will shift your focus from you to someone else. As you read over the next few days, listen carefully to the heart of The Father and those who cry out through the written words.

Open your heart and take time each day to pray for someone besides yourself. This stage will truly examine, test, and expose your heart.

DAY THIRTY-SIX: ALL THAT GLITTERS IS NOT GOLD

All that glitters is not gold...

How many times in your life have we heard that little idiom? Six little words yet together they have such a powerful meaning.

We are reminded that just because something looks valuable or real on the outside does not mean that is what you find on the inside. This can apply to so many things.

Growing up in Jersey, we had meat markets. You could go to the supermarket to buy meat, but the best place to go was the meat market.

Moving around throughout the years, I still hang on to going to the meat market and attempt to find one where ever I land. When I do, I can go to this place and get EXACTLY what I need.

The area I currently reside, this has become quite the challenge. There are so few REAL meat markets, and you really have to search to find one.

Recently, after leaving an appointment, I drove by this place with this HUGE sign. It was a meat market. Wow, I can finally get what I really need, but for some reason, I did not stop to go in. Next time I am this way, I thought, I will make that stop. Meanwhile, later, I went to look up this particular place online. I was surprised at what I found.

The place that came up online, same name, was in a different location. Interesting...

The next time I am in that area, I did not stop again. Why are things happening that deter me from making this stop? Next time, for sure...

Then again, in that area but I was not thinking of stopping yet I ended up having to take a detour that allowed me to get to this place.

Ok, let's check it out...

The first thing I notice that I did not see previously...There is a fence surrounding this place. Considering the location, that was surprising. In fact, this fence made it very difficult to see every aspect of what was happening on the outside of the building.

Then, attempting to locate the entry point, was worse but after a few turns and asking God, what is the world this was all about?" I found my way.

So, I pull up in the lot, and the first thing you see are junk cars, severely damaged and abandoned vehicles, but there are a small number of decent vehicles.

I pull up, put my car in park, step out of the vehicle and prepare to head in (as I am praying and asking God why I have not just turned around yet). Before going in, I stand there and take one more glance over the lot where all these vehicles are just parked. You can tell they have not moved in a very long time.

All of my senses tell me what's inside is not what is on their sign. I also came to realize that there must be something I am supposed to see. Therefore, I proceed with caution.

I slightly open the door and immediately see EVERYTHING besides anything to do with meat. Items, stacked up that you can tell were not used in a very long time. They served no purpose anymore...just sitting on a shelf. Some items were heavily damaged...even looked burned up.

I did notice a man sitting in the back at a desk...He was working.

Within seconds, I was back in my vehicle and headed off the lot.

Now, what does this all have to do with anything? It goes back to the idiom, all that glitters is not gold.

Just because there was a huge sign outside of the building stating it was a meat market does not mean it was a meat market. This place was evidently being used for other than what it was intended.

Unfortunately, this has happened with some of our churches or places of worship and people who make up the body of Christ.

You really need somewhere to go that will provide you with "meat." You need God's word to feed you. Finally, you make your way to a place to get fed and unfortunately, there is a fence on the outside.

The fence is protecting this place, so the people who put it up believe. The TRUTH is, the fence has pretty much kept you out. It has indeed become a barrier because you are trying to figure out…How do I get in?"

Nonetheless, you keep pressing to just get to this place. Then you see all the vehicles that were abandoned. They are just sitting there and serve no purpose. Even the land around the site is unkempt or cared for. There is no sign of LIFE even on the outside.

The OLD items stacked and stored inside are just on a shelf. They no longer have value or purpose. Even the building is run down. It is "dim" inside and quite frankly, it just looks a bit shabby.

Where is God?

Surely He is not here, for IF He were, then what matched on the outside would be on the inside.

If He were there, then there would be LIFE on the outside AND the inside.

If He were there, then what you came to get would be there.

If He were there, there would be a place for you at the "table" to be FED.

Instead, when you looked inside, there sat a man in the back, behind all the rummage, in dim light. This MAN, even when you appeared, took no notice but kept going on with whatever he was doing before you arrived.

TRULY, this is not where you are supposed to be. There is no need to continue to move toward the inside. There is no need to move into a place where darkness prevails, and there is nothing to sustain you.

There is no need to sit in a place that has become trashed and no longer representing what it says on the outside.

What must be done is to go back and discover the place that is not perpetrating to be something it is not.

What must be done is to find the RIGHT place. The place that you found having the same name BUT it was in another location. That place has, on the inside, everything that is advertised on the outside.

That place is authentic through and through.

It is crucial that as God continues to move, we are moving WITH Him.

It is vital to our lives that we stay connected to places that represent God and His Word.

We must understand that just because the "sign" says something that does not always mean the interior matches.

Know that EVERYTHING that glitters is not gold.

Everything that has a little flash or excitement does not have WORTH.

Remember, you can hear something that sounds good because others are getting excited, but if you stop for a moment, not allowing yourself to get caught up/distracted by excitement, you may just HEAR something that lets your HEART know, "This is NOT right."

When settlers came to this country during the gold rush, and others migrated in search of gold. What many found was what they referred to as, "fool's gold."

What's the difference?

Gold is a natural metal while Fools gold is not.

Gold does not give off an odor. Fool's gold contains sulfur. (Sulfur smell is very offensive. It resembles that of a rotten egg)

Gold is soft and malleable. Like, true believers and leaders, it can be shaped and molded allowing for continued transformation. Pyrite (Fool's gold) is brittle. It will shatter when hit. Much like when you have a stony heart. Something happens, and you fall to pieces because there is nothing there to help you hold together. This, therefore, impacts how you will deal with others. It may explain outbursts, fits of rage/anger rather than love.

When Real gold is rubbed against something, it leaves a mark that resembles its characteristics. It would leave a [light] yellow mark. When fool's gold rubs against something, although the outside of it is yellow, the mark is leaves is a dark green or black color. Gold leaves light, but the fool's gold leaves darkness.

Fool's gold will glitter when exposed to light BUT has no shine to it. Therefore, it cannot shine in the darkness. Gold, on the other hand, has a pure luster and can be seen even in darkness. It stands out and brings light into darkness. Light drives out darkness.

As we to seek to grow in the things of God, we MUST not mistake fool's gold for gold. It is imperative that we are able to tell the difference when entering in or connecting with people and/or places of worship.

Check the characteristics of where you are, who you are connected with, who is rubbing off on you. Ensure you have GOLD.

If not, then all that you thought was worth something, will leave you holding weight when trying to stand before The Lord. You will want to be seen and recognized for Light recognizes light and rises above darkness, BUT you will have been weighed down by all the ROCKS, that all you were able to do is sink.

In Revelation 2:18-23, John addresses the church of Thyatira, with the Word of The Lord.

Here we see that The Son of God has taken notice of the works done by the church; HOWEVER, He holds them accountable for their corruption. The church, the bride of Christ, has taken on a new bride...Jezebel.

Fresh Manna: Journey To A New Beginning

No longer in alignment with Christ, this church has displeased The Lord for allowing things to happen that are contrary to God. False teachings exist, controlling situations, and the "food" delivered to the people is NOT clean. The food was meant for something other than what it was being used for. This was not food prepared for God's people.

The warning has been made. Christ has spoken, and those who chose to stay with this church will receive the same consequences.

Thinking that perpetration is something God will tolerate is unacceptable. There is no way we can live as a body, claiming to Love God, claiming to be reconciled with Christ, yet still "in bed" with those who live contrary to His ways. We cannot believe that we can just sit in a place where the TRUE Unadulterated Word of God is not taught. If we think we are supposed to come in week after week only to hear a feel-good message that allows you to stay in your place of comfort rather than piercing our hearts and inciting change, then we are mistaken. Yes, God is LOVE, but Love is also sometimes giving much-needed correction. Love wants you to change, grow, and become better and NOT stagnant.

Known as The Corrupt Church, they are warned that they will receive according to their actions. See, what was in their hearts was not God for if He were, then there would be no need for Christ to reiterate to them that "ALL the churches shall know that I am He who searches the Heart."

Apparently, they forgot...Apparently, they thought that all the outward things they were doing were enough to "pass." Seems the thought was they could hide, mask, cover-up, dress-up, disguise, what was inside by what was on the outside.

The heart and minds are searched. Just because you dress it up in gold does not make it gold. The Lord sees through it ALL. While people are running around playing dress-up to seem righteous, or getting up every week to "play church" The Lord, sees that it is all an AFFAIR.

He recognizes FOOL'S GOLD perpetrating as GOLD and as His people, so should we (if He is who we are following).

It is written that those who Keep His Works until the end shall receive His promises. They shall be privileged to rule and reign in His kingdom, as coheirs.

It is in these times that we need to STAND and CHOOSE whose side we are on....Who we want to remain connected with...where we are planted.

Where do you stand? Are you open in your heart and connected to Christ, able to recognize truth...able to see the heart?

OR

Are you still falling for the FAKE STUFF, thinking that all that glitters is gold?

Reflections:

1. Where do you stand? Are you the light in a dark room or do you blend in?
2. Do your actions rub off on others, allowing them to be led further into the light or in darkness?
3. Can others tell if you are gold (genuine) or the fake stuff? Can you tell? What makes you different from anyone else?

DAY THIRTY-SEVEN: THE ADVOCATE

Who will be a voice for the voiceless;
a people who have longed to be heard
Who will stand in the gap for them;
to ensure they are not just kicked to the curb

Who will be so daring
as to stand above those who are less caring
seeing the needs of others before their very own
Speaking out and coming to the aid of those left alone

In more ways, than we realize, we can all affect change
Learning to see the world around us but not just
through our eyes
We need to see through the eyes of the estranged

Carefully, when we listen to the stories untold
we can be a voice for those left in the cold
Sometimes helping to reshape the heart and minds of
those around us
we are making an impact to help others be more
prosperous

Many times we go searching high and low around the
world
seeking to be the voice of a lost boy or girl
But what about those in our very backyard
the neighbor, family member...those we can reach by
walking, phone or car

Advocacy is not something you need a grand platform
to stand on
You basically just need to be present physically and
emotionally as a shoulder to stand on

For as you take the low road, paving the way,
you are allowing them to stand up and see just how far
they can go
You are allowing them to see they are and were,
NEVER left alone

Today's Challenge:

As you go about your day focus your attention on the world around you, rather than your personal needs. Take the time to listen to others. Do not be in such a rush. Allow the Holy Spirit to guide you and be a light for someone today.

Extend kindness, compassion, love, and understanding. If the opportunity presents, extend prayer. Be a voice for someone as you stand in the gap for them speaking to God on their behalf. You can do this even without them knowing.

At the end of your day, reflect on your actions and interactions. Reflect on how you felt emotionally, physically, and spiritually.

DAY THIRTY-EIGHT: LOVE THY NEIGHBOR

When I think of my neighbor, who do I see?
Are you my neighbor because you look like me?
Are we a community because we share the same blood
or are we a community that is joined together by love?

When I see you do I see me;
or can I see you clearly to see your needs?

Caught up in my day to day activities
The suffering surrounds me in the midst of their calamities
But I move on collecting my wealth
failing to contribute to their mental, physical, and spiritual health

The poor sleep on the streets
but all I am concerned with are my personal needs
Christ wants us to care for one another
yet, I still cannot see you as my sister or brother

You're nothing more than one begging for help
all I see is you failing to help yourself
If I can learn to survive on my own
creating wealth and building a huge home
Then why must I give to the lazy
the poor, drunk, dumb….are you crazy?

I have worked hard to get to where I am
And I fail to give to you on the corner
This is nothing but a scam

I have read reports on the news

Fresh Manna: Journey To A New Beginning

About you phonies who are just begging to get the newest pair of shoes.

I will not take out of the mouths of my family
To give to the one who is nothing but a leach and a phony

When Sally or Joe from next door comes to my stoop, I shall give openly
but to you bum on the corner, I have not mercy

For they look like me and live as I do
But for you, on the corner, I am nothing like you
They are my neighbors, and to them, I shall give
But as for you
Are you not my neighbor...
Am I not obligated to help you
For you do not live where I live

Today's Challenge:

As you go through your day, take a moment and give a little more of yourself than usual, without expecting something in return. Extend love and mercy to a stranger, someone in need. Rather than turning away or driving by that same homeless person you see every day, buy them a cup of coffee and or a meal, speak a blessing to them.

Find the opportunity to give your time. Look for an opportunity to volunteer in your area. Go read to children, run errands for a sick or elderly neighbor. Perhaps, there is a family in your area that could use help. Babysit for a neighbor and give the parent(s) a break.

Reflect how this makes you feel and why? Why are these actions important to God? What did you learn about yourself and those you helped?

Fresh Manna: Journey To A New Beginning

DAY THIRTY-NINE: THE REFUGEE

What shall you have of me;
When everywhere I turn, I face opposition to be free
What shall I do to live;
When all who see me say I have nothing to give
I am torn down looking for a home
Walking around this great land all on my own
Will I ever find a place to belong?

What shall become of me;
When I have no voice, unable to speak freely
All that I have ever learned
Is so dear to my heart
But the place I have come wants to tear it all apart

I left my home, my people and all of my friends,
Coming here to find hope, joy, and make amends
I am looked upon as different and in some ways a danger
I just want to find a new life but like you Lord, yet my family and I were sent to a manger

Everything I thought this journey would be
A life of peace and finally some prosperity
Has this been all in vain;
For they have treated me poorly since I came

I just want to finally be free
I left my land thinking, here I would be free indeed.
Once a prisoner, and now a stranger
Where is my help, Father? My help from all harm and danger?

Rather than taking the time to understand me,

Fresh Manna: Journey To A New Beginning

> I am feared, misunderstood, and left alone
> Your word says that we are to live in unity
> But when will I get to experience the manifestation of your ministry?

Today's Challenge: Bridging the Gaps

Spend time getting to know someone from a different background than you. Where are they from? What were their experiences growing up? Their family life? Challenges they face? How is their life different from yours? How is it the same?
Do you have more in common than you initially realized?

Reflect upon what makes you different but also similar. What did you learn? Have you learned to be more open minded? Do you have more compassion and empathy for those different than you? Why is this important to God?

DAY FORTY: SANCTUARY

The storm was coming, there was a raging of the sea
You began preparations to flee, but what about me

While you could afford to pack, getting ready to go
Many were left stuck, left alone in their home

You were fortunate enough to have the means to escape
While some are barely living paycheck to paycheck
So, they stayed, rationing what they had and barely ate

Huge airports and churches, stood empty and desolate
While way too many suffered without the proper provision needed to survive.
Many made it out alive, while others, were left to die

Where are the churches in the people's time of need
Leaving God's children in the hands of the government
What about the poor, the children, and the elderly
Those with nothing or scraping means together as they live off social security

Many times they are giving more than your greatest donors or tithers, whom you celebrate and praise
But these are the ones making the greater sacrifice in what they gave
Yet they go unnoticed, passed over, and too often left in the cold
No one has taken the time to listen to their stories untold

Fresh Manna: Journey To A New Beginning

Just as those, who call themselves the church, has turned their backs on them
The day shall soon come when you shall be cast away from HIM

See, you have gone from creating a place that you call HIS home
To worshipping all that is wrong, and desecrating the throne

When positioned correctly, with our hearts lifted up and ears open
would you not be able to provide the need before the need just as Christ did for you and me
Would you have been able to provide a place of refuge from the storm
By using God's House as a dorm

Consumed with the money invested in the structure and all that lies within
Protecting the building because this is the only true place of worship
While all along preaching that God shall provide all that you need
Yet the church stands firm without being an integral part of the community
I guess what is within the walls is only for whoever enters in on Sunday Morning
Despite what is said, it really is not a place for those really suffering

Who is the CHURCH protecting if those who are in need is kept outside of the gate?
But to those who have made barricades, in the end, are you the ones He will SAVE

Today's Challenge:

How are you being a safe place for others, showing love, compassion, and allowing vulnerability?
Can you love and accept people where they are, to allow them to grow in Christ or do you judge them at a first glance?
Do you listen with the heart of God or your preconceived thoughts of what someone's life should reflect?
Do you condemn the broken without understanding their story and first providing love?
Are you welcoming and inviting, or do you shun the hungry, lost, hurt and broken?

As part of today's church, who are you providing a safe place for and how?

EPILOGUE

After His baptism, Jesus spent 40 days and 40 nights in the wilderness. Just before coming out and entering into His ministry, He was tempted by the adversary (satan).

Three times satan tempted Christ, yet Christ stood firm in knowing who He was and who He belonged to and rejected satan. He chose to side with THE FATHER. As you have come to the end of your journey, you too must decide who you shall stand with.

My prayer is that you have found encouragement, strength, and faith in your journey. I pray that you have spent time getting to know God and will continue to grow with Him.

CHOOSE YE THIS DAY...

THE ENTRANCE EXAM

Are you standing in the Light or standing in the dark
For you cannot stand in both as they are worlds apart

Will you choose to live or will you choose to die
For you cannot have both, yet if dead you can be revived

Will you choose to be bound or will you choose to be free
For you cannot do both; so, what shall you ask of Me?

I shall give you what is in your heart

Choose Ye this day
What does the heart say
Do you want to be with Me
Or have you chosen the adversary

Fresh Manna: Journey To A New Beginning

ACKNOWLEDGEMENTS

Thank you to those that have prayed along with me to get this book completed and into the hands of those who need it.

Special thank you to my cousin, Cristal L. Randolph for designing the perfect cover for this book. You captured what was in my head. To my friends Kathy Lofton, and Oluwasina Awolusi for your support and belief in the vision.
I pray God's continued Blessings in your life.

About the Author

Shawanda R. Randolph retired from the United States Air Force after 20 years of service. God would use her keen sense of wisdom, insight, and innate leadership skills, to help guide, direct, and influence those around her. It was her discipline, worth ethic, and problem-solving skills that led both superiors and fellow associates to seek her counsel. As, a result, many flourished under her advisement and mentorship. Even then, she understood that it was God who gave her the wisdom and desire to guide others to walk their God-given paths in and outside of the military.

God would use her life as a model, propelling her to teach others the important realization that their spiritual, professional and personal life was interconnected. This would become the foundational concept of her ministry: Identity.
She knew that once people began to see themselves through God's eyes, they would unlock their true potential and lead a more fulfilled life.

Shawanda holds an MBA in Health Care Administration from Wilmington University and is currently pursuing a Master's in Theology and Ministry with Fuller Theological Seminary. She is the proud mother of one exceptional son.

For continued inspiration and words of wisdom, subscribe to her blog, "Fresh Manna." Fresh Manna's mission is to nourish the soul of the lost, replenish those who have accepted Jesus into their hearts, and build God's next generation of leaders.

www.ingramcontent.com/pod-product-compliance
Lightning Source LLC
Chambersburg PA
CBHW071916290426
44110CB00013B/1375